# ISLAY SCENES

Diana Leitch graduated as an architect with a thesis on the history of Islay's distilleries, before joining the practice of Ian Lindsay, a leading exponent in the restoration and revitalisation of Scottish architectural heritage. She then pursued an academic career at Newcastle University School of Architecture, where she served as Head between 1997 and 2002. Home is Islay and drawing is always an act of discovery.

*Front cover: Lochindaal Distillery*
*Back cover: Bowmore*
*Illustrations by Diana Leitch*
*Cover design by Shakira Campion*

# ISLAY SCENES
## PORTRAIT OF AN ISLAND

DIANA LEITCH

ORIGIN

First published in 2025 by
Origin, an imprint of
Birlinn Limited
West Newington House
10 Newington Road
Edinburgh
EH9 1QS

www.birlinn.co.uk

Text copyright © Diana Leitch, 2025

Illustrations copyright © Diana Leitch, 2025

Design and typesetting by LexisBooks

The moral right of Diana Leitch to be identified as the author of this work has been asserted by her in accordance with the Copyright, Designs and Patents Act 1988

All rights reserved. No part of this publication may be reproduced, stored or transmitted in any form without the express written permission of the publisher

ISBN: 978 1 83983 093 8

British Library Cataloguing-in-Publication Data
A catalogue record for this book is available from the British Library

Printed and bound by Bell and Bain Ltd, Glasgow

# Contents

| | |
|---|---|
| Preface | 1 |
|     An Enduring Transformation | 2 |
|     Appreciating the Past | 3 |
|     Isolation and Ingenuity | 4 |
| Islay House estate | 7 |
| Sunderland estate | 41 |
| Ballinaby estate | 47 |
| Kildalton estate | 53 |
| Dunlossit estate | 65 |
| Farms and steadings | 71 |
|     Farmhouses | 73 |
|     Farm steadings | 86 |
| Villages | 93 |
|     A village house | 94 |
|     Bowmore | 96 |
|     Port Ellen | 98 |
|     Port Charlotte | 100 |
|     Port Wemyss | 102 |
|     Portnahaven | 103 |
|     Keills | 104 |
|     Ballygrant | 105 |
|     Bridgend | 106 |
|     Port Askaig | 107 |
| Churches, manses and schools | 109 |
|     Churches | 111 |
|     Schools | 125 |
| Mills and distilleries | 129 |
|     Linen (lint) and woollen mills | 130 |
|     Cereal crop (grain, meal) mills | 133 |
|     Distilleries | 134 |
| And a small but significant building ... | 144 |
| In conclusion | 146 |
| Bibliography | 148 |

*Port Charlotte beach and lighthouse (completed in 1869 and designed by David and Thomas Stevenson).*

*To Felix and Cassius*

# Preface

My quest to better understand Islay's built heritage began with my parents' renovation of our house in Port Charlotte, one of many buildings abandoned but nonetheless regularly whitewashed by those who cared deeply about the inherited character of their village. Appreciation of the ways in which houses, farm buildings, churches, schools and, most surprisingly, the relatively bulky distilleries sat with timeless elegance in the island's rugged landscape was to shape my thinking both as an architect and as an academic.

My search for how and why these buildings came to be so visually rewarding led to friendships with Freda Ramsay, custodian of the Kildalton estate papers, Dr Margaret Storrie, whose tireless research enabled her authorship of *Islay: Biography of an Island*, and Rona Mackenzie, who shared my enthusiasm for recording village life. More recently, looking into my own family background and exploring the origins of the buildings and landscapes around me through drawing led to an increasing respect for those responsible for Islay's remarkable architectural heritage.

The idea behind publication came from Colin Roy at The Celtic House in Bowmore but could not have been realised without generous support from the Mactaggart family and the Dunlossit and Islay Community Trust. I am also indebted to the current occupants of Islay's delightful buildings who gave so freely of their time and knowledge.

I have always enjoyed expressing myself in drawing, but not so much in writing. So I am forever grateful to my nephew David Cook, my sons Nick and George Wharton and my husband Tony for a healthy combination of encouragement and criticism.

Finally, as an admirer of those behind the ongoing success of the Museum of Islay Life – not least Malcom Ogilvie and Les Wilson – I am dedicating this book to the museum for its benefit in the years to come.

Diana Leitch
Islay
June 2025

*Port Charlotte from the south.*

# An Enduring Transformation
## *Shaping the Island of Today*

Islay has been subject to continual change. Neolithic farmers, Iron Age settlers, clan dynasties and, in the twentieth century, the infrastructure of war have all left their mark, but the way the island looks and works today stems primarily from the eighteenth and nineteenth centuries. The impact of Georgian and Victorian ambition was to be of exceptional significance.

The most substantial transformation came with those who amassed fortunes elsewhere, such as the Campbells of Shawfield who bought much of the island in 1726. Their story, along with those of other landowners, is one of grand ideas and aspirations: some realised, some thwarted, and all reliant on implementation by islanders who had little choice but to build and farm as directed.

Other significant influences on island life during this period came from national and international developments. Changing attitudes to religion, education, agriculture and industry all left their mark and contributed to a legacy that characterises the island, one that remains legible in both buildings and landscapes.

# Appreciating the Past
## *Drawn Reconstruction*

Much of Islay's heritage is in robust shape, but where this is not the case, appreciating the past depends on piecing together archival material, such as written accounts, maps, artists' impressions and old photographs, and matching it with surviving physical evidence. Individual memories have also been vital to the narrative of this book.

Buildings are drawn accurately and in a consistent manner, so as to enable stylistic comparison and appreciation of ideas embodied in their structure. Other more scenic sketches enable understanding of the contexts at the time of their building, views that would have been familiar to eighteenth- or nineteenth-century eyes.

Of the examples chosen, most are privately owned, but can be seen without the need for intrusion. The dangerous ruin of Kildalton Castle is an exception, as it lies almost totally out of everyday sight and is inaccessible.

*Port Charlotte from the sea.*

*The dunes of Loch Gruinart looking towards Corryvreckan, the whirlpool between Jura and Scarba.*

*Rocks at Lossit bay on Islay's Atlantic coast.*

# Isolation and Ingenuity
## *Extreme Weather and Scarce Materials*

The Hebridean island of Islay lies off the south-west coast of Scotland, the last landfall at the edge of the Atlantic Ocean.

Pebble beaches, left high and dry after the last ice age, a thick blanket of peat bog laid down by ancient plant life, and sands blown into dunes, are all evident on the surface of the ancient rocks which rise out of the sea. Few patches of native woodland survive and, despite their age, the windswept trees remain small and contorted.

The gneiss rock at the south-west tip of Islay is amongst the oldest in the British Isles. None of the substructure of the island is newly laid down, and even the most recent varieties of rock have been hardened by the intense heat of the Earth's core, some moulded into striated waves.

*Lime-washed harling masks the roughly hewn local stone of eighteenth and early nineteenth-century Georgian windows.*

*Finely worked imported sandstone frames a late nineteenth-century Victorian window.*

The first builders on Islay relied on found materials, such as heather, grasses, dried peat, loose stone, coppiced tree stems and driftwood. This continued to be normal practice up until the seventeenth century, except where places of worship or the residences of the ruling elite required a greater presence and finesse befitting their status. For these, various local stones were quarried: some for taller and straighter walls; some for roofing slate; and some to be burnt in a kiln, then ground down to make lime for a bonding mortar.

For the most prestigious buildings, materials such as the more easily carved sandstone needed to edge doors and windows and the more substantial timbers needed to span bigger spaces, were imported as far back as the twelfth century.

In the eighteenth and early nineteenth century, the limited availability of suitable materials remained a significant factor in determining what could be built, as did the island's exposure to extreme weather conditions. The relatively small, rough Islay slates required a steep pitch to shed the wind-driven rain. Roofs and walls had to meet without overhang, so as to avoid wind uplift.

Without mechanical tools, the dense local stone was difficult to cut and shape into precise blocks. Crevices were unavoidable, even with walls nearly a metre thick. Harling added a protective outer layer and it was common practice to use it for some Islay buildings in the early years of the eighteenth century. Harling was an aggregate of small pebbles, shells and sand mixed into lime mortar and reinforced by animal hair, so as to avoid it cracking. Regular coating of the harling with lime wash maintained weather resistance.

Materials which had to be imported, such as sandstone, timber and glass, were a pricey status symbol. Until late nineteenth-century developments in glass manufacture, panes were limited in size and this resulted in the subdivision of window frames.

The widespread use of imported materials came with the building of new villages in the early nineteenth century. Even at that time, all were used sparingly, and despite an improvement in transport links as the century progressed, access to the ever-increasing range of materials available elsewhere on the mainland was to remain the preserve of the wealthy on Islay.

*Successive Islay House lairds shaped their immediate estate and the island as a whole. The implications of their projects for the island's economy, society, settlements and landscapes remain evident to the present day.*

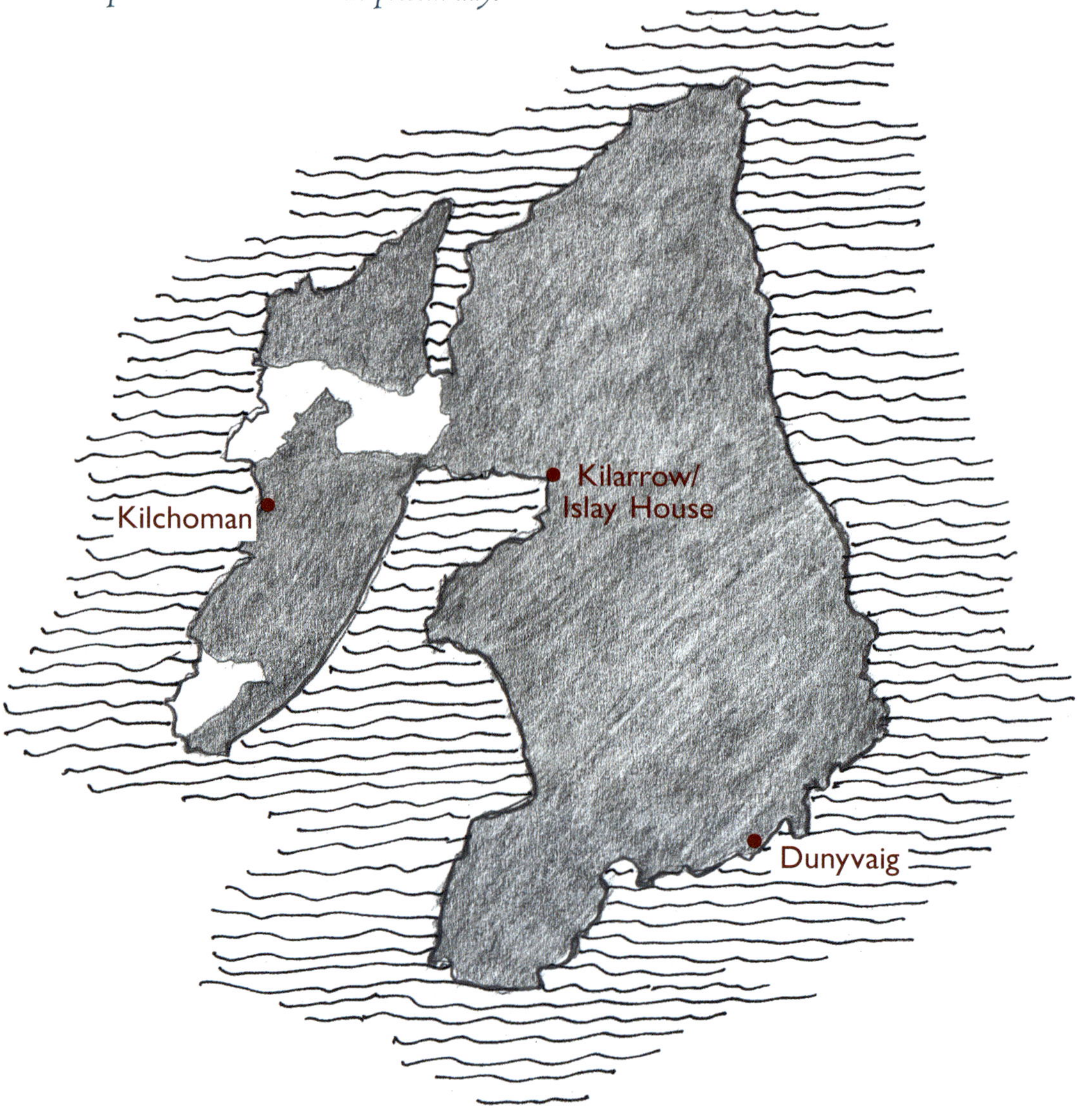

 *Islay House estate in 1726.*

# Islay House estate

*The ruins of Dunyvaig Castle, Lagavulin.*

Until the seventeenth century, those who wished to retain control of their lands on Islay sought naturally defensible locations and built in expectation of siege.

For several centuries Islay played a pivotal role in establishing, maintaining and then eventually relinquishing an independence shared by Scotland's islands and western seaboard with parts of the north of Ireland. Lying at the geographic heart of these territories and ideally placed to command the interlinking sea corridors, a rocky outcrop guarding Lagavulin Bay on the east coast of Islay became a key defensive location. Dunyvaig was named after and sheltered the much-feared 'nyvaig', a fighting vessel developed from the Viking longboat. Possibly first fortified in the twelfth century, Dunyvaig was a seat of considerable power in the early fourteenth century, when the lengthy period dominated by the Clan Donald 'Lords of the Isles' began.

The eventual downfall of the MacDonalds was long drawn-out and bitterly contested. Although they had lost outright supremacy by forfeiting much of their entitlement to James III of Scotland in the late fifteenth century, they managed to cling onto effective control until the early seventeenth century.

In 1614, James VI of Scotland, substantially empowered by his succession to the English throne as James I, provided military backing to the Campbell clan who had long been building a power base in mainland Scotland. Together they sought to oust the MacDonalds once and for all. As part of the campaign, a naval bombardment devastated Dunyvaig. The island inherited by the new ruling elite, the Campbells of Cawdor, was reported to be a wasteland.

*Kilarrow (now Islay) House and the nearby settlement of Kilarrow at the head of Loch Indaal.*

There were further skirmishes throughout the first half of the seventeenth century and, as long as feuding remained a threat, none of the incoming Cawdor landowners, or lairds, spent much time on the island. Dunyvaig was only partially rebuilt, and used primarily as an administrative base. The first of the Cawdor lairds to spend longer periods on Islay was Sir Hugh Campbell. Initially he favoured a former MacDonald base at Kilchoman on Islay's west coast and made this his residence. Then, in April 1677, after a period of relative calm, he commissioned a grand new home.

Whilst adopting the pragmatic characteristics of earlier castles in terms of strategic location and potential robustness when under attack, Sir Hugh also built with an eye on comfort and elegance. He chose a site at the centre of the island, and built a tall L-shaped stone house, commanding panoramic views of Loch Indaal. This still stands, as the central structure of the present Islay House.

Shortly before starting on their Islay residence, Sir Hugh and his wife Isobel had substantially rebuilt the north and west wings at their ancestral seat, Cawdor Castle in Nairn. Both this and their new Islay home were three-storied and L-shaped, with steeply pitched slate roofs. Both used stone quarried locally, mostly as roughly coursed rubble, but with more crisply cut stone edging to doors, windows and the 'crowstepped' gables. Given the timing and similarity in both form and construction of the two houses, brothers James and Robert Nicholson from Nairn are likely to have been the masons responsible for the new Kilarrow House on Islay.

Investment in this grand residence was followed by the establishment of the nearby administrative and trading settlement of Kilarrow, which lay between present day Bridgend and Islay House. Today all that remains of the settlement is the graveyard. Everything else was demolished to make way for the eighteenth-century pleasure gardens of Islay House, and Kilarrow was replaced by the new town of Bowmore.

In the early eighteenth century the Campbells of Cawdor ran into financial difficulties, exacerbated by a devastating cattle disease, and in 1726 were forced to sell their lands on Islay to Daniel Campbell of Shawfield.

*The seventeenth-century Kilarrow House built by Hugh and Isobel Campbell of Cawdor, drawn in similar style to their recently completed reworking of Cawdor Castle. The newly established commercial and administrative settlement of Kilarrow clustered around the medieval parish church and was separated from the laird's mansion by an artificial lochan probably dating back to an earlier monastic settlement.*

*Shawfield House, Glasgow, built in 1712 and designed by Colen Campbell as a demonstration of the stylistic rules set out in his* Vitruvius Britannicus.

The new owner of the Islay lands, Daniel Campbell, had accumulated his wealth as a youthful maritime entrepreneur trading in iron ore, tobacco and the brutal transport of slaves. He was to be the first of his family, the Campbells of Shawfield, to significantly reshape the economic and social development of Islay, as well as its built and cultivated landscape.

The name 'Shawfield' came from an estate in Lanarkshire, an early acquisition. In fact, Daniel's family originated in Argyll, and it was there that he built on his commercial successes and established his status when elected to the Scottish Parliament in 1703. As member for the Burgh of Inveraray he developed a close relationship with the Campbell Dukes of Argyll.

In 1712 Daniel, newly elected as representative for the Glasgow Burghs in Westminster, commissioned a new home to accommodate his household in Glasgow and assert his position in society. His architect was Colen Campbell (coincidentally nephew of Sir Hugh Campbell of Cawdor), a Scot by birth but with an expertise drawn from time spent travelling in Italy.

In addition to his architectural practice, Colen Campbell produced a series of volumes entitled *Vitruvius Britannicus*. Vitruvius was a first-century BC Roman architect, engineer and author of *De Architectura*, in which he recorded the buildings of Greece and Rome, linking them to theories on how to achieve the essential architectural qualities of *firmitas*, *utilitas* and *venustas* ('strength', 'utility' and 'beauty').

Vitruvius taught that

*Beauty is produced by the pleasing appearance and good taste of the whole, and by the dimensions of all the parts being duly proportioned to each other.*

*Proportion is that agreeable harmony between the several parts of a building, which is the result of a just and regular agreement of them with each other; the height to the width, this to the length, and each of these to the whole.*

In the fifteenth century, *De Architectura* was a fundamental source of inspiration for Renaissance architects such as Leonardo da Vinci, providing an insight into classical form and detailing, as well as proffering ideas about symmetry and proportion.

In the sixteenth century the Venetian architect Andrea Palladio produced *I quattro libri dell'architettura*, in order to disseminate Vitruvian thinking to a new generation. It was this publication which inspired seventeenth-century British architect Inigo Jones, most notably in his new Banqueting House for King James, by now the joint monarch of England and Scotland.

It took until the eighteenth century for classically inspired architecture to reach the rest of the British Isles, and Colen Campbell's reworkings of Vitruvius and Palladio played an important role in popularising the style which became known as Georgian (i.e. coinciding with the reigns of the first four Hanoverian Kings from 1714 to 1830).

Pre-dating the Georgian New Town of Edinburgh by 50 years, Shawfield House was undoubtedly influential in shaping Scottish architecture. Included as an exemplar in *Vitruvius Britannicus*, it epitomised the characteristics fundamental to achieving the timeless Georgian townscapes we continue to admire today.

In 1725 Daniel Campbell fled from Shawfield House with his family, the night before it was attacked by rioters objecting to his support for a tax on malt which increased the price of beer. In 1745 the house was reputedly used by Prince Charles Edward Stuart to meet his mistress. It was demolished in 1792.

The Shawfield Campbell family moved to their other property, Woodhall House in Lanarkshire. It too was damaged in the riots, but was refurbished (probably by Colen Campbell), and became their home until the mid-nineteenth century. It was demolished in 1924.

 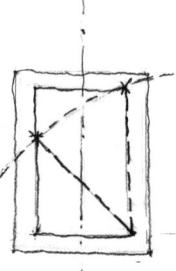

*Window height is equal to the diagonal drawn from the bottom corner.*

 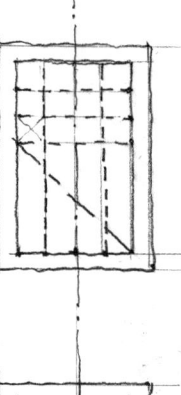

*Window height is equal to the width plus three-quarters of the width.*

 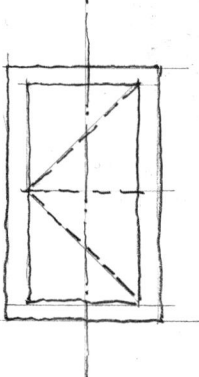

*Window height is double the width.*

*The windows in the new west wing of Islay House in relation to the ideal proportions set out by Andrea Palladio in* I quattro libri dell'architettura.

On Islay the new laird commissioned a reworking of the existing Kilarrow House to comply with the latest Georgian aesthetic. He added a new wing and altered existing windows. The result was a near-symmetrical façade, with aligned windows decreasing in height from ground to roof.

In the absence of a stone suited to carving the finer details of Greek or Roman temples, achieving classical styling on Islay relied entirely on proportional relationships that reflected their architectural inspiration. The rough-textured local stone would have detracted from the desired effect, so was hidden beneath a smooth layer of lime-washed harling. Imported sandstone was used sparingly to edge and emphasise the carefully calculated geometries.

Daniel renamed his new home 'Islay House', and it heralded the way in which buildings, be they grand houses, farms or whole villages, came to embody consistent Georgian characteristics, creating a distinctive and coherent elegance.

The Georgian interest in classical civilisation was not limited to aesthetics. The period which became known as the Enlightenment, saw a holistic re-engagement with classical thinking, which was founded on direct observation of the world and the universe in a way that predated what were considered to be the stultifying effects of medieval religious ideology. Daniel shared an enthusiasm for this new way of thinking with peers such as the 3rd Duke of Argyll, and one aspect of it that interested both men was the creation of highly planned settlements.

Impressed by the architecture of London and Bath, the 3rd Duke of Argyll worked up a draft proposal for a new town next to his ancestral seat at Inveraray, the first to be envisaged in Scotland. In addition to securing William Adam, a leading exponent of Georgian ideas, as his architect, the Duke founded his plans on the latest theories about how communities might function. Inveraray was to promote a civilised society and act as a catalyst for diverse employment. On Islay, Daniel too was busy with an ambitious plan for a new town to replace Kilarrow, one that would exemplify Georgian elegance and stimulate economic growth.

Changes were also afoot in the wider landscape of the island, where Daniel aimed to increase agricultural productivity and to develop other industries such as mining, fishing and linen production, thus simultaneously benefiting the islanders and capitalising on his investments.

Changing agricultural practice was to prove particularly challenging. Allegiance to a clan chief had long assured that access to farming rights was passed down through the generations, creating a fragmented landscape cultivated for survival rather than profit. Although it was not achieved in his lifetime, Daniel initiated the transformation which eventually uprooted families and reallocated the land, creating the farms that we see today.

For his accomplishments, as much as for his physical stature, the first Shawfield laird became known as 'Great' Daniel Campbell.

*'Great' Daniel Campbell's Islay House remodelled in 1737 from the earlier Kilarrow House.*

*The now ruinous church of Kilarrow amongst the new two-storied houses of an emerging merchant class. The stepping-stones across to Islay House were repaired in 1755.*

*Woodhall House, Lanarkshire in the 1750s.*

In 1753, 'Great' Daniel Campbell died aged 83. He was succeeded by his 16-year-old grandson, also called Daniel and therefore referred to as 'the Younger'. Inspired by his grandfather's vision and enabled to act by inheriting wealth, the new laird relished the chance to apply the latest thinking about agriculture, industry, town planning and architecture to his own projects. His architectural plans were most certainly informed by his travelling on the Grand Tour. This opportunity of studying the ruins of classical civilisations was an experience he shared with John, Lord Lorne, the 5th Duke of Argyll, increasing the likelihood that they discussed their various projects between them.

In 1768 Daniel the Younger set about the building of Bowmore, the new town envisaged by his grandfather. Practical constraints and scenic potential both played a part in the choice of site. For the venture to succeed, a navigable shoreline for commercial shipping was essential, and this located the development on the loch side to the south-east of Islay House. The precise siting then looks to have been determined by the landscape. Placing the distinctive profile of Bowmore's lime-washed buildings along an inclined ridge served to accentuate both the natural shape of the landscape and the town's apparent grandeur. From Islay House this arrangement could be seen to best advantage, in profile. The laird could enjoy a view enhanced by his fine new town.

Placing the settlement at some distance from Islay House brought other advantages, not least the uninterrupted enjoyment of the landscape around the mansion. With Kilarrow no longer on the doorstep, extensive woodland could be planted, both affording privacy and sheltering the more exotic planting required by the latest trends in pleasure gardens. An ornamental lake replaced the marshy lochan.

In 1760 the young laird had also begun works to Islay House itself. As a bachelor, he found the accommodation adequate for his needs, but lacking in fashionable elegance. Drawing on his time in Italy, the work of Andrea Palladio and aspects of the Shawfield residence of Woodhall, the design of Islay House was elaborated by the addition of two identical stair towers. The angular polygonal outer forms enclosed the most graceful of circular stairs, lit at each level by the three light windows, typical of Palladian styling.

*Islay House in the 1780s, with the new town of Bowmore in the distance and lush planting around an ornamental lake in place of the former settlement of Kilarrow.*

*Daniel Campbell the Younger's Islay House and landscaped gardens in 1770.*

*In the 1770s the existing house at Eallabus was 'put in good condition'.*

*Samuel Crawford's grave in Kilarrow cemetery.*

Set in the new woodland plantation to the north of Islay House, another relatively grand mansion was also taking shape. There had long been a house on the site at Eallabus, home to the 'baillie' or estate manager. The incoming occupant of the new Eallabus was a well-respected surgeon called Samuel Crawford. His home was to be the first three-storied house on the island, apart from Islay House itself, and was generously embellished with classical motifs in finely crafted sandstone.

Eallabus clearly met with Samuel's approval and he stayed on, becoming the new estate manager, by now known as a 'factor'. His son, John Crawford, was to achieve international fame. A physician like his father, he was also a linguist and, as a diplomat, became best known as an early administrator of Singapore.

*Daniel's last building. Although on the site of a gun emplacement, the battlemented tower was built to scenically adorn the new garden.*

The celebrated Welsh traveller, zoologist and antiquarian, Thomas Pennant, wrote a detailed account of his short visit to Islay in the summer of 1772. This and other contemporary records offer a snapshot of the extent to which Daniel Campbell the Younger succeeded in fulfilling his grandfather's ambitious plans.

In terms of agriculture, Daniel was to be overly optimistic. His estimate that nine-tenths of the acidic, peaty island landscape could be transformed by treating the soil with shell-sand, lime, manure and seaweed was to prove unrealistic. Despite this disappointment, Pennant and others noted a marked increase in yields where land improvement had been combined with new crop types and crop-rotation.

Incentives aimed at attracting a skilled workforce to revitalise other industries were also put in hand. Islay had a long history of producing linen from flax, fishing and lead-mining. In addition, Daniel supported the manufacture and export of kelp, a seaweed transformed by burning into a key ingredient in the manufacture of glass and soap.

*The entrance to Islay House Square's Home Farm.*

*The walled gardens date from this time, and, presumably to amuse his 13 children, Walter built a menagerie for exotic animals.*

On his death in 1777, Daniel Campbell the Younger was succeeded by his brother Walter. The new laird was to spend relatively lengthy periods on Islay, and oversaw substantial development. By the 1790s, Islay boasted 30 miles of roadway, with stone bridges, two quays, regular sailings to the mainland, and increased export trade in cattle, horses, fish, kelp, linen yarn and even grain. In Bowmore, the first sizeable distillery opened for production in 1779, and the new town was also attracting specialist craftsmen, such as weavers, masons, joiners, smiths and saddlers.

At Islay House, it was Walter who established the Home Farm to further agricultural development by way of example. The new farm buildings formed a courtyard and included living quarters and workshops. Seen from Islay House, it presented a typical Georgian façade, with identical two-storied wings flanking a pedimented entrance archway, complete with clock turret and belfry.

*Despite his sizeable family, Walter made few changes to Islay House itself. He did however commission a handsome new doorway, framed by finely carved buff sandstone to emulate classical antiquity.*

Nearby, on the Islay House estate, the comparative grandeur of a new factor's house featured similar sandstone detailing to that of Walter's doorway. Daill sits in the fertile valley to the north-east of Islay House and was the location of a noted residence well before the advent of the Shawfield Campbells. Previous residents, kin of the Cawdor Campbells, played prominent roles in the politics of their time.

In the mid-nineteenth century, Daill was to become the residence of William Webster, the overseer who administered the estate following the departure of the Shawfield Campbells. Webster is particularly remembered for taking control of the lands around his home, evicting the tenants and using former arable acreage to graze sheep. Although common elsewhere in the Highlands and Islands by this time, the widespread introduction of sheep was a new development for Islay.

By the time the Islay House estate had found a buyer, the incoming laird noted that Daill, rather than Islay House, would have been his preferred Islay home had he intended residing on the island. In the event, William Webster stayed in his role as overseer and in his home.

Whilst the stonework of the house at Daill demonstrates the refined elegance of Georgian high society, the masonry of its sizeable steading exemplifies the unadorned robust beauty of local materials and craftsmanship.

*The late eighteenth-century estate factor's house at Daill, replacing (probably incorporating) an earlier version.*

*The farm steading at Daill.*

*An earlier house, extended and elaborated for the Islay House gardener. Each stone gatepost was topped with an urn decorated with heraldic beasts.*

When Walter died in 1816, he was succeeded by his 18-year-old grandson, Walter Frederick, the 4th and last of the Shawfield Campbell lairds. Walter Frederick's era lasted for 32 years, during which time the transformation of Islay continued apace, creating much of the character for which it is known today. The villages of Port Ellen, Port Charlotte and Port Wemyss were designed to further diversify opportunities for employment. All were firmly Georgian in style, both in their organisation and the character of their individual buildings.

As the Georgian period progressed, so did the exploration of aesthetic appeal, the relationship between built form, context and the mind of the viewer. Landscape painters became a source of inspiration, as grand gardens mimicked pastoral settings and influenced the placement of even the most modest buildings. The pleasing, picturesque siting and individual character of the estate workers' houses from this period, which frame and line the routes around Islay House, demonstrate these aesthetic considerations. In one example, as if to emphasise the sweeping curve at the head of Loch Indaal at Bluehouses, an earlier two-storied house was elongated and elaborated by the addition of two symmetrical wings.

In 1837 Victoria began her long reign and, by the time she commissioned her beloved Balmoral Castle, the contrast between her new Highland home and the buildings illustrated in Colen Campbell's *Vitruvius Britannicus* was vividly evident. With a visual complexity that suggested gradual evolution rather than a singular architectural design, Balmoral's asymmetry was embellished with a variety of window types and elaborate turrets.

This new formal variety enabled a building's exterior to reflect its interior workings, rather than hiding everything behind a uniform façade. This theme of honest expression extended to the way in which materials and construction were now placed on display, even dramatised.

The ideas behind Balmoral had been rehearsed in the 1820s by Sir Walter Scott at Abbotsford, his home on the River Tweed. As he built he drew on his familiarity with myths, legends and their medieval settings, the Scottish fortified tower house in particular. The Scottish Baronial style had arrived.

By 1840, architecture which celebrated a sense of place, national identity and a somewhat romanticised view of history, was widespread. The abrupt and radical stylistic shift required of architects was exemplified in the work of William Henry Playfair. It was Playfair who created the classically rigorous Georgian architecture at the heart of Edinburgh, most significantly the National Gallery of Scotland and Royal Scottish Academy. Then, mid-way through the 1830s, he embraced the new Victorian style with aplomb. An early example of his versatility survives at Stonefield Castle in Tarbert. Built for John Campbell in 1837, Stonefield would have been well known to the Islay Shawfield Campbells.

In 1841 Walter Frederick called on Playfair to extend Islay House with a mix of single- and two-storey ancillary accommodation, more than doubling the floor area of his mansion. The resultant juxtaposition between the calm whiteness of the existing Georgian house and the restlessness of its vibrantly colourful neighbour retains the ability to surprise and stir the senses.

Although intended to be evocative of place and history, this first example of Scottish Baronial on the island is more likely to have been viewed as exotic and alien. The complex forms and imported red sandstone would have seemed even more extraordinary then than they do today.

*The front (above) and rear elevations of Walter Frederick Campbell's Islay House in the 1840s.*

*The back door to Islay House with Walter Frederick Campbell's monogram.*

Nostalgia for the heroism of past times, the new freedom to personalise architectural embellishment and a desire to be immortalised, saw men such as Walter Frederick signing their creations with medieval heraldic style monograms, typically on doorways and gatehouses. The Islay House monograms survived, but this was to be Walter Frederick's last project. The problems facing Islay by the 1840s were part of a wider malaise in the Highlands and Islands. On Islay, even the improvements in agricultural yields and the development of settlements around alternative industries could not meet the demands of the ever-growing population (which had more than trebled to around 15,000 since the days of the first Shawfield laird).

Changing the traditional ways of the islanders had been gradual. Many families remained dependent on sharing the produce from their small inherited plots, even as their numbers swelled. Their poverty was exacerbated by adverse weather events and the potato blight: islanders went hungry, rents went unpaid and the Shawfield Campbells went bankrupt.

In the autumn of 1847, Walter Frederick's son, John Francis, attempted to salvage the Islay estate. His efforts were in vain, and from January 1848 until August 1853 the Shawfield Campbells' lands on Islay were administered by Edinburgh accountants. A broken man, Walter Frederick lived out his final years in Normandy, where he died in 1855. His black marble sarcophagus in Bowmore's round church lies empty.

In 1853, James Morrison, reputed to be amongst the wealthiest men of the time, with extensive property including residences at Fonthill in Wiltshire and Basildon Park in Berkshire, became the new owner of the Islay House estate. In effect, it was the ageing James' son Charles who took on the task of running the estate. This he did by employing managing factors. Charles did visit Islay but never lived there. However, he was primarily a businessman and kept a very close eye on the financial side of island affairs. James died in 1857.

Those who bought into the Scottish Highlands and Islands in the latter part of the 1800s did so mainly in pursuit of picturesque, unspoilt wilderness and sporting opportunities, made highly fashionable by writers, artists and their queen. Charles Morrison did not fit this stereotype and looked to support the type of economic growth that would sustain the island community, as well as ensuring a return on his investments.

*The East Lodge gate house to Islay House with Walter Frederick Campbell's monogram.*

By the latter part of the century, market prices for exports, such as the highly regarded Islay black cattle, had picked up. The fishing industry had expanded, the island distilleries were thriving and the move towards large, more viable farms had accelerated. Many impoverished islanders had emigrated. Between 1830 and 1850, the population had fallen by about 4,000. For those who remained, investment in the construction of new roads and buildings offered additional employment.

The ambitious scale of the Shawfield Campbells' interventions had given the new owner of Islay House an enviable degree of economic stability. In addition, the estate welcomed new employment opportunities, such as herring-processing on the shores of Loch Gruinart and new distilleries in Bruichladdich and Bunnahabhain. Apart from contributing to the island's infrastructure, Charles Morrison had no need to build other than modest accommodation and facilities for his new tenant farmers and estate employees. He certainly saw no need to waste money on renovating Islay House, which he considered to be inconveniently large.

The death of Queen Victoria in 1901 ushered in an Edwardian era characterised by a divergence in architectural tastes. Whilst some continued to enjoy the High Victorian preference for combining a variety of styles in a busy, eclectic mix, others favoured a return to the relative calm of classical architecture. Others again sought to eschew superficial stylistic influences and looked for inspiration in materials and craftsmanship, a movement that became known as Arts and Crafts.

The start of the century also marked a new era on Islay. Charles Morrison died in 1909. The new owner, Hugh Morrison, was married to Lady Mary Leveson-Gower, granddaughter of Walter Frederick Campbell, and the couple immediately appointed an architect to remodel Islay House to suit their lifestyle and aesthetic preferences.

Their architect, Detmar Blow, had a reputation for the sensitive restoration of historic buildings, and his early commissions favoured the honest expression of the emergent Arts and Crafts movement above those of Georgian classicism, where conformity to an idealised appearance took precedence.

It would seem, therefore, that the classical lookalike Islay House transformation was driven chiefly by the clients' aesthetic inclinations. That said, the new three-storied nursery wing satisfyingly echoed the materials, geometries and subtle proportions of its neighbour, whilst the lower eaves height helped to make it visually subservient. However, the new addition did make it more difficult to distinguish and, therefore, to appreciate the Georgian original.

*William Playfair's Victorian exuberance is all the more surprising now that it is discovered only by going round to the back of Islay House.*

*Hugh and Mary Morrison's Islay House in 1915 with a new neo-Georgian façade screening Walter Frederick Campbell's early Victorian wing.*

*Sunderland estate was formed in the seventeenth century by combining the lands of Cladville, Sunderland, Foreland and Coull. The Campbell lairds introduced agricultural reform on the estate and created the village of Portnahaven.*

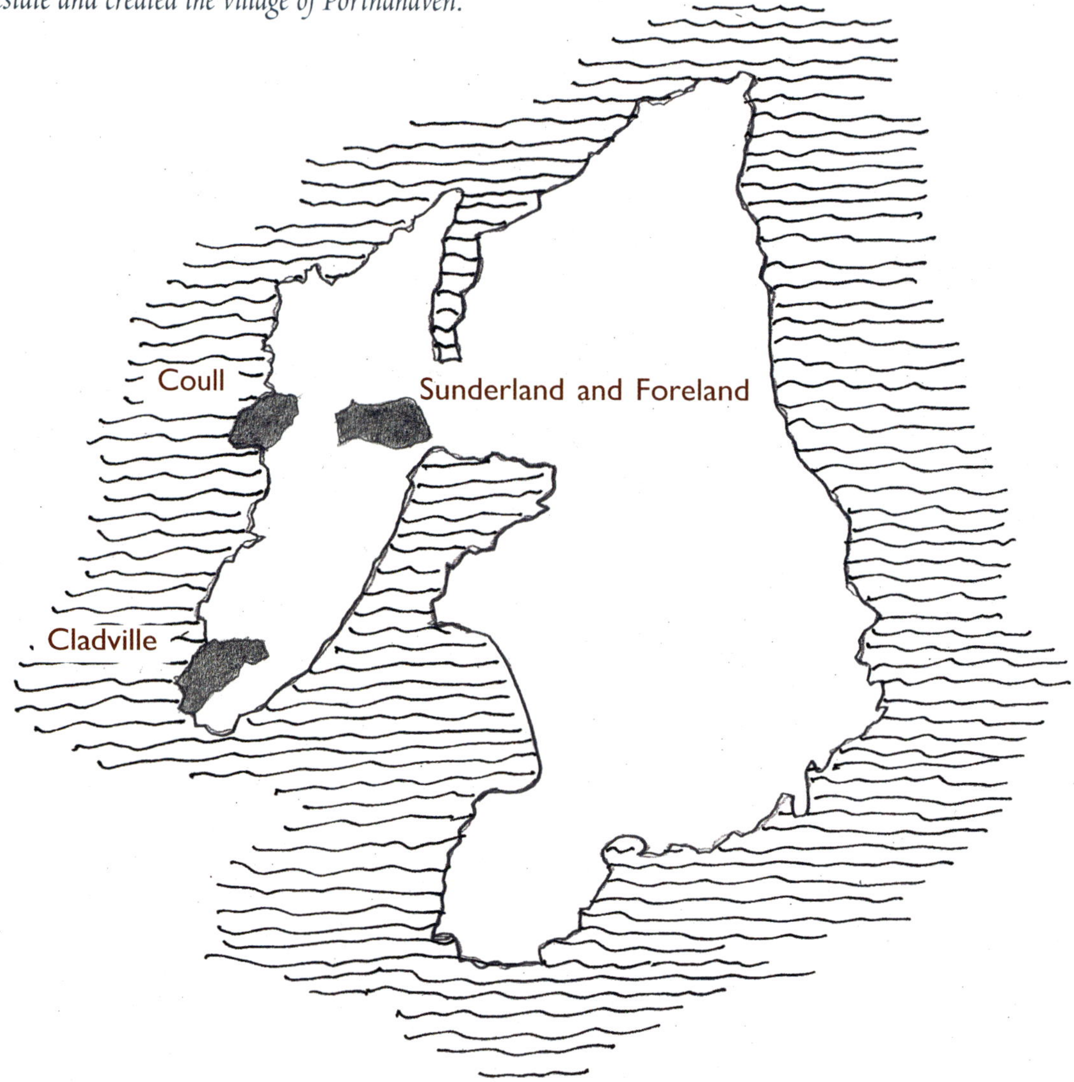

*Sunderland estate in 1772.*

# Sunderland estate

*The sheltered gardens of Foreland House.*

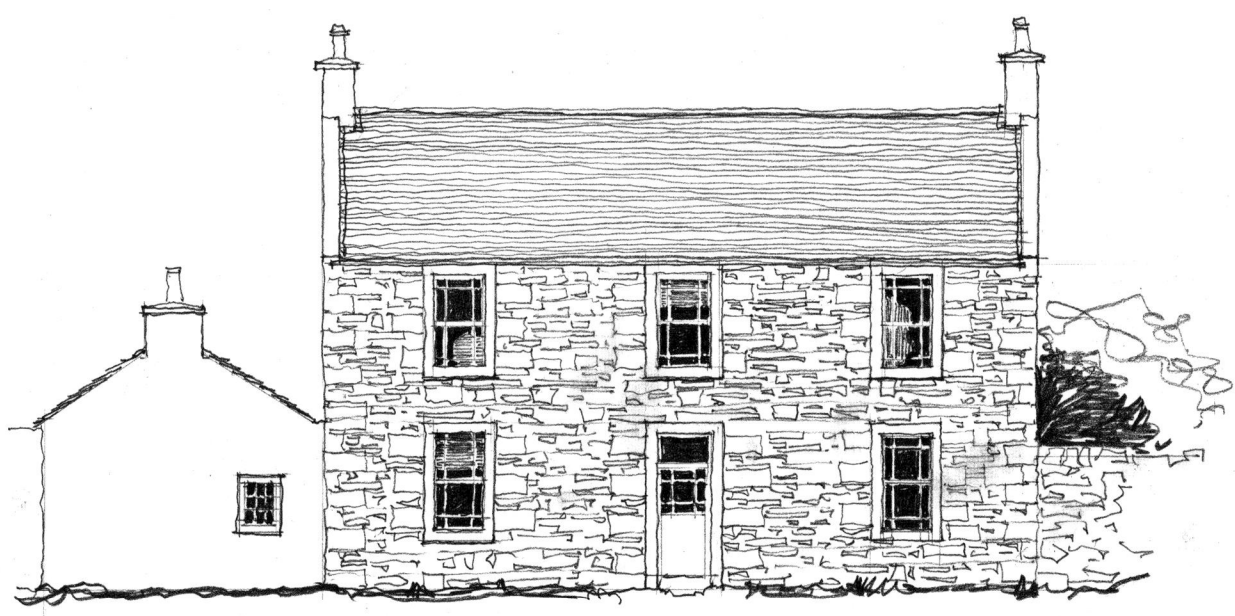

*The nineteenth-century Sunderland farmhouse sits beside the earlier eighteenth-century house.*

In July 1772, the inquisitive naturalist and antiquarian, Thomas Pennant, spent three nights on Islay. The first was spent with Charles Freebairn, manager of Islay's mining industry, the second with the Campbells of Sunderland, and the third with the Campbells of Ballinaby. He also dined with Daniel Campbell the Younger at Islay House.

The Sunderland estate at the time consisted of three distinct parcels of land. One lay on Islay's west coast, to the north of Kilchoman Bay at Coull. The second combined the lands of Sunderland on the south-eastern shore of Loch Gorm and those of neighbouring Foreland. The third lay at Islay's south-western tip, and included the lands of Cladville and the village of Portnahaven.

The separate ownership of the Sunderland estate was rooted in the 1500s, as powerful clans jostled for power. On Islay, animosity had been building between the MacDonalds and the Macleans, both of whom claimed possession of land, including that centred on the island stronghold of Loch Gorm. In 1598, a particularly savage battle on the shores of Loch Gruinart saw the Macleans defeated by the MacDonalds, but, by 1614, the latter had also been displaced by a new laird, Sir John Campbell of Cawdor. Between 1614 and 1628, it was one of Sir John's kin, Colin Campbell, who was first granted Cladville and then Sunderland, Foreland and Coull, becoming the first of the Campbells of Sunderland, one of Islay's most influential families.

Thomas Pennant clearly enjoyed the hospitality of Robert Campbell, the last of the Cawdor lineage to own the estate. The visitor wrote enthusiastically about what he saw as exemplary improvements, such as increased productivity in farmland and investment in the fishing industry. He also noted the fine quality grass and Sunderland's sheltered apple orchard.

The present-day house at Sunderland dates from the mid-1800s, but is adjoined to one side by the earlier single-storey house where Robert Campbell would have entertained Thomas Pennant. This may look far from grand, but on his death in 1780, Robert left a collection of books, silverware, five crystal decanters, two copper coffee pots and a 'domestic' copper whisky still.

In 1788, Walter, the third of the Shawfield Campbell lairds, added the Sunderland lands to his Islay House estate. At the north-eastern edge of his new estate he took on a remarkably ambitious enterprise, the drainage of Loch Gruinart's extensive wetlands. This would prove an exceedingly long-term project. Even after changing the flow of freshwater towards Loch Indaal and constructing a sea wall, a system of drains had to be laid across the whole area. The final part of the scheme fell to Walter's grandson, Walter Frederick, and it was his successful government grant application in the 1830s that paid for a factory to produce drainage tiles. The remains of the factory still stand to the north of Foreland House.

By the time Walter Frederick inherited the Islay House estate in 1816, Sunderland had been re-established as a separate estate. In 1814 ownership had passed to his uncle, a former Captain in the East India Company, also called Walter. It was the new Sunderland laird who chose Foreland, at the north-eastern tip of his estate, as the ideal site for his principal dwelling. Two-storied and elegantly proportioned, the doorway of the main house was embellished with finely carved sandstone columns and a pediment. The comparative grandeur of this house was created by its depth, essentially

*The Georgian house at Foreland flanked by the kitchen/servants' quarters and additional reception rooms.*

two pitched-roof houses back-to-back, forming a valley along the join. This enabled generously windowed rooms to be arranged either side of a gallery space running the length of the joining spine.

To one side of the main house, a long, low kitchen and servants' wing was remodelled from an earlier core, possibly the original dwelling recorded on the site in 1750. To the other side a billiard room and conservatory completed the grouping.

Captain Walter Campbell of Sunderland showed the same enthusiasm as his nephew, Walter Frederick, for reshaping the landscape and buildings on his estate, including the reconstruction of the fishing village at Portnahaven, but his lands were to suffer as badly from the catastrophic events of the 1840s as the Islay House estate. In 1846 the Sutherland estate passed from the Shawfield Campbells to Glasgow merchant Alexander McEwan. In 1851, the new owner wrote to his MP seeking support for, amongst other things, investment to revive Islay's flax industry. He reported that over 120 acres of flax were growing successfully on his estate, and the flax mill, behind the farm at Sunderland, continued working until the latter years of the century. Sadly, given his optimism, Alexander McEwan was Laird of Sunderland for only a short time after sending his letter. By 1861, the Sunderland estate had been split amongst several owners.

Over the years, Foreland House, its gardens and surrounding woodlands were much extended and although not on the same scale as Islay House, Foreland is undoubtedly a gracious home with a fine horticultural heritage.

*Ballinaby estate was granted to the Macbeth (also known as Beaton) family in the fifteenth century. It flourished under a series of Campbell lairds until Ballinaby House was devastated by fire in 1933.*

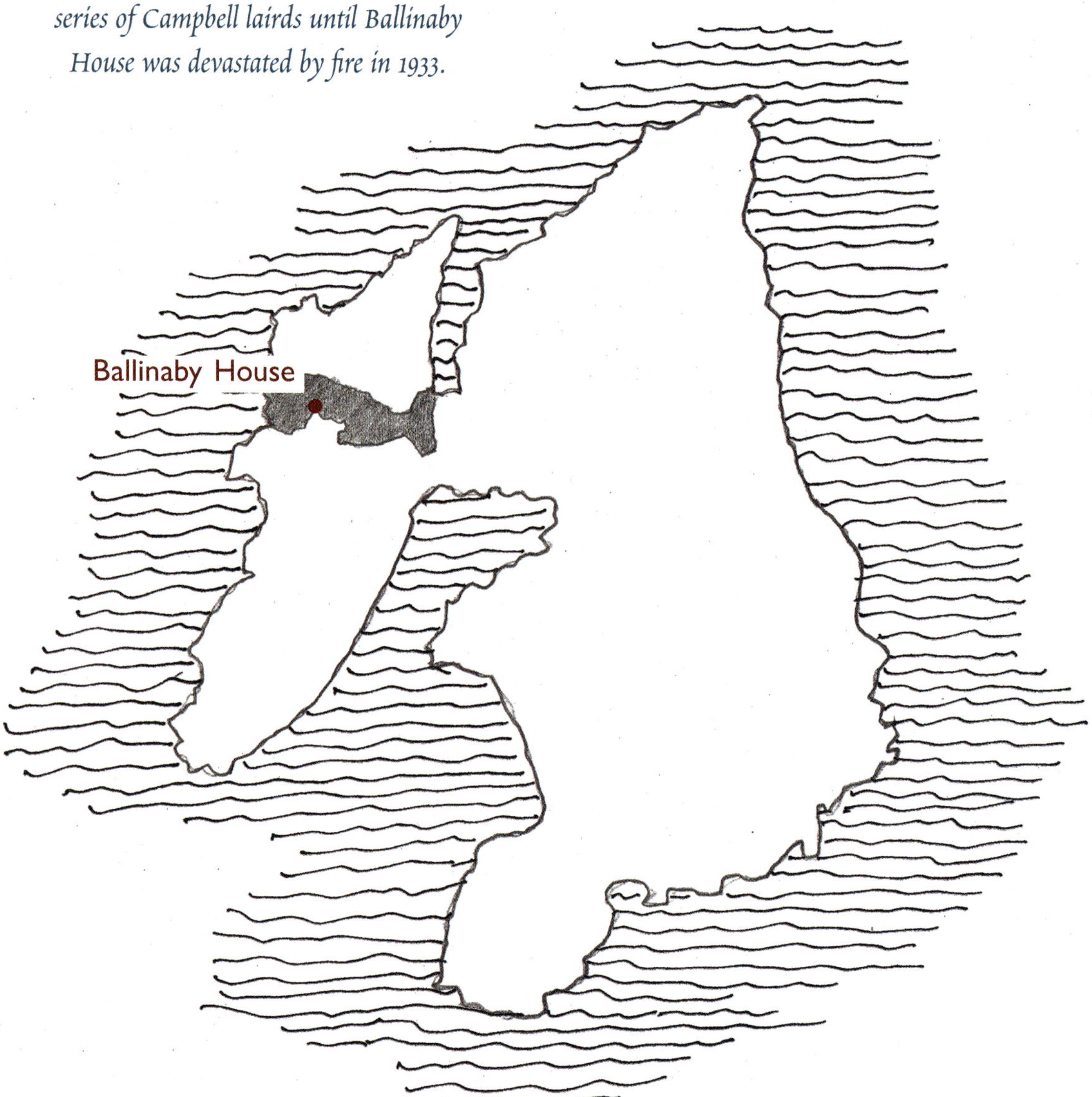

 *Ballinaby estate in 1772.*

# Ballinaby estate

*Ballinaby House, the walled garden and steading on the north bank of Loch Gorm in 1900.*

The estate of Ballinaby, visited by Thomas Pennant in 1772, consisted of a narrow, fertile strip running inland from Saligo Bay on the Atlantic coast to Loch Gruinart in the east. It bordered the Sunderland estate and Loch Gorm to the south.

As a separate estate, Ballinaby can be traced back to the 1400s, when it was linked to the MacBeth (also known as Beaton) family, physicians to the MacDonald Lords of the Isles. In 1609, entitlement to these lands was confirmed by King James VI in recognition of Fergus MacBeth's elevated status as chief physician in the islands.

In 1629, Fergus's son John sold the estate to Lord Lorne (later Earl and 1st Marquis of Argyll), who granted it for a fixed rent (known as a feu) to kin of the Islay House Cawdor Campbells. The Campbells of Ballinaby were to become one of the most prestigious Islay families. An inventory from the early 1700s lists collections of glass and silverware, and a map drawn up by George Langlands for John, Duke of Argyll, towards the end of the century sees fit to name only two Islay gentlemen next to their residences, '*W Campbell Esq of Islay House*' and '*Don Campbell Esq of Ballinaby*'.

Thomas Pennant was as complimentary about the farming practices at Ballinaby as he had been about both Islay House and Sunderland. At Ballinaby he noted the improving effects of spreading shell-sand to encourage grass growth on formerly barren heath, and was favourably impressed by the early hay harvest as well as the quality of the new potatoes served up for his dinner.

Dinner would have been hosted at Ballinaby House. Built around 1750 and modest in comparison to Islay House, the original Ballinaby nonetheless stood taller and wider than any other building on the island at the time. In line with Georgian principles of symmetry and proportion, a tall gabled wall emphasised the central entrance bay.

Ballinaby estate changed hands again in 1778, passing to another Campbell family, also principal tenants of neighbouring farmland. In 1811 the *General View of the Agriculture of the Hebrides*, prepared for the British Board of Agriculture, was to echo Pennant's endorsement of the farming practices at Ballinaby and included specific praise for the quality of working horses bred on the estate.

The estate of Ballinaby continued to prosper throughout the century. The house was enlarged, an extensive walled garden was created and an impressive farm-steading was built, including housing for several carriages.

*'Ballinaby House burnt down every one safe.'*

     McLachlan, Post Office Telegraph,
     Bruichladdich, 9.45 a.m., 16 June 1933.

*Ballinaby House as it looked prior to the devastating fire of 1933.*

  By the 1920s, Ballinaby became widely known because of its association with Harry Lauder, a singer and entertainer who attained worldwide fame and legendary status in his own lifetime. A close friend of the Ballinaby family, Angus and Matilda McLachlan, he was having tea in the house in June 1933 when fire broke out.

  After the fire the house stood as an empty shell until the end of the Second World War, when it was blown up by the army as they cleared ammunition stores before leaving the island's military bases.

*The steading and walled garden as seen from the front of Ballinaby House in 1900.*

*The Ballinaby steading clock tower of 1891.*

*Created in the mid-nineteenth century by the newly established Morrison lairds of Islay House, the Kildalton estate was sold to John Ramsay of Port Ellen distillery, who invested in new roads and ferry services, as well as building projects.*

Cairnmore House

Kildalton Castle

Port Ellen

 *Kildalton estate in 1861.*

# Kildalton estate

*Ardimersay Cottage, Kildalton.*

In the autumn of 1847, when the Shawfield Campbells of Islay House faced bankruptcy, Walter Frederick's son, John Francis, looked to a trusted family friend, John Ramsay, for advice and support.

As an 18-year-old, John Ramsay first came to Islay in 1833. He arrived at Port Ellen distillery to work there, introduced through family connections, and, although uncertain about his future, he quickly warmed to whisky production. He was to be instrumental in reviving the fortunes of the distillery, and played a significant role in improving agricultural practice.

His success was recognised by the then Islay House laird, Walter Frederick Campbell, who transferred the lease and, later, ownership of the distillery to the young man. Then, in 1853, when the Islay House estate was finally sold, John Ramsay struck up a productive working relationship with the new owner, Charles Morrison. Specifically, they collaborated to expand the island's road network, harbours and ferry services.

Charles Morrison was well aware of the problems of unprofitable land usage that had beset the Shawfield Campbells, and could see the advantages of selling off those parts of the estate with the least promising prospects of cultivation. Between 1855 and 1861, John Ramsay became owner of the newly formed Kildalton estate, an area which stretched down the east coast of Islay from Proaig (north of Ardmore on the Sound of Islay) to the tip of the Oa and across to Laggan Bay.

Faced with the extreme hardships of the mid-century, over a quarter of the islanders had emigrated, and others had been forced off the land to seek work in the new villages. The relatively barren uplands of the Oa were an exception, and in remote valleys, clustered communities (known as 'townships' or 'townlands') remained rooted in their traditional ways. Decisions about their future now fell to John Ramsay. His solution was to offer financial support to encourage emigration. Between 1862 and 1863, it is estimated that several hundred took up his offer and left for Canada. Although he justified his actions by voicing concern about the constant threat of starvation to island life, he clearly remained troubled by his role in this, travelling out to Ontario to check on the displaced islanders.

John Ramsay made his first home on Islay at Cornabus farm, close to Port Ellen distillery. Then, when he married in 1857, he and his wife Eliza moved further up the east coast to Ardimersay Cottage at Kildalton. Built in 1825 by Walter Frederick Campbell, Ardimersay was not intended as a home, but rather as a whimsical setting for relaxed entertainment after a day's shooting.

Alongside Georgian society's drive to learn from the physical world, grew a desire to engage more playfully with nature. Cottages such as Ardimersay, evidently rooted in a long-established folk tradition rather than the formal architecture of Islay House, became the height of fashion in aristocratic circles. However, the sweeping roof of finely trimmed reed thatch and intricate timber trelliswork of Ardimersay clearly was derived from the English home counties, ensuring that it was not seen as an actual rustic cottage, but as a highly designed artificial representation of one. Interestingly, its characteristics such as masking an upper floor within the roof form and the borrowing of materials and detailing from age-old traditions, not necessarily local ones, were to make a lasting impression on British domestic architecture.

Ardimersay's location on Islay's east coast would have been deliberately chosen for scenic effect and was much loved by the Ramsays. When Eliza died in 1864, John stayed on at the cottage, but its construction was not well suited to the Islay climate. By 1870, the now wealthy John had replaced the cottage with a grand new residence to which he brought his second wife, Lucy.

*Kildalton Castle and its landscaped gardens in 1870. It had fallen into to ruin by the mid-twentieth century.*

This new home, the imposing Kildalton Castle, epitomised the Scottish Baronial style favoured by the new Victorian landowning elite. The now sparsely populated hills and lochs across Scotland were much sought after for their sporting potential. A new era of grand houses combined roughly hewn exteriors evocative of past heroism, together with interiors offering the latest luxury, perfect settings from which to experience the 'savage wilderness'. At Kildalton the precisely cut stone was deliberately textured to give an appropriately rugged effect, whilst the interior boasted a state-of-the-art bathroom with a shower.

Essentially comprising two main parts (one of two storeys, the other of three) either side of a tall tower, Kildalton appeared to be a much grander house than this scale of accommodation might suggest. The formal subdivision of the blocks, the steepness of the crowstepped gables, the exaggerated height of the chimneys, the tower split into two parts, all combined to create a restless upward silhouette which enhanced its apparent size and grandeur.

Windows were varied in style, displaying a virtuosity made possible by the latest developments in sheet-glass production and allowing the distinct function of each part of the house to be 'read'. Size of windows indicated the scale of the space being lit, whilst style denoted relative status. This honesty of expression played well to the Victorian sense of morality. The architect, John Burnett, had recently designed Auchendennan Castle on the banks of Loch Lomond for John Ramsay's father-in-law, George Martin. As a wealthy East India Company merchant, Lucy's father had been able to build in similar style, but on an even larger scale and more elaborately.

*Kildalton Castle entrance. The variegated stonework, attributed to John and Donald Spalding, emphasised the manner of its construction.*

*A gatehouse marks the south-western threshold to the Kildalton plantations.*

John Ramsay initiated a range of infrastructure projects of benefit to the island's economy, both during construction and after completion. At Kildalton, for example, he not only invested in his own residence, but he also undertook an ambitious construction project to house his many employees.

A series of highly individual estate houses were designed to punctuate the route past the entrance to Kildalton Castle itself. Whereas the smaller cottages of the Islay House estate had closely matched the contemporary styling of the main house, those of Kildalton seemed to go out of their way to differ from one another and from anything else on Islay.

On the one hand this can be understood as a celebration of the stylistic freedom which increased as the nineteenth century ran to its end. On the other hand, the variety seems intent on showcasing the potential to be found in a multiplicity of building materials. Each material has been used to best advantage, and the quality of workmanship has mostly withstood the ravages of time. The relationship between the character of each cottage and its exact siting also looks to have been carefully choreographed. It is hard to imagine any of them swapping location.

Immediately to the north-east of Ardbeg, the broadly spreading terracotta roof of a small roadside cottage guards what was the entrance to the more private and lushly planted landscape around Kildalton Castle. An iron gate stands ready to close the road and a revolving pedestrian gate, hidden within the stone walling, hangs from a semicircular iron arch to one side.

At times hemmed in by woodlands, at times breaking out onto the rocky shore, the road beyond this gate is reputed to have been the inspiration behind a song written in the wake of the First World War by acclaimed Scottish entertainer, Harry Lauder, who, as mentioned earlier, was a regular guest at Ballinaby House. The lyrics of 'Keep right on to the end of the road' speak of facing life after loss. The Lauders' only son, John, was killed in action in 1916 at the age of 25.

A little to the north of the gatehouse, the narrow road passes through the dense plantations of Kildalton Castle. Marking the entrance driveway to the main house is the most enchanting of cottages. Built out of Islay quartz, it glistens brightly against the dark woodland. The red-tiled roof of the original L-shaped lodge overhangs, to rest on a colonnade of intricate timber lattice posts. These are identical to (and most probably salvaged from) the colonnade at Ardimersay Cottage, evoking a fond memory of the Ramsay's first home.

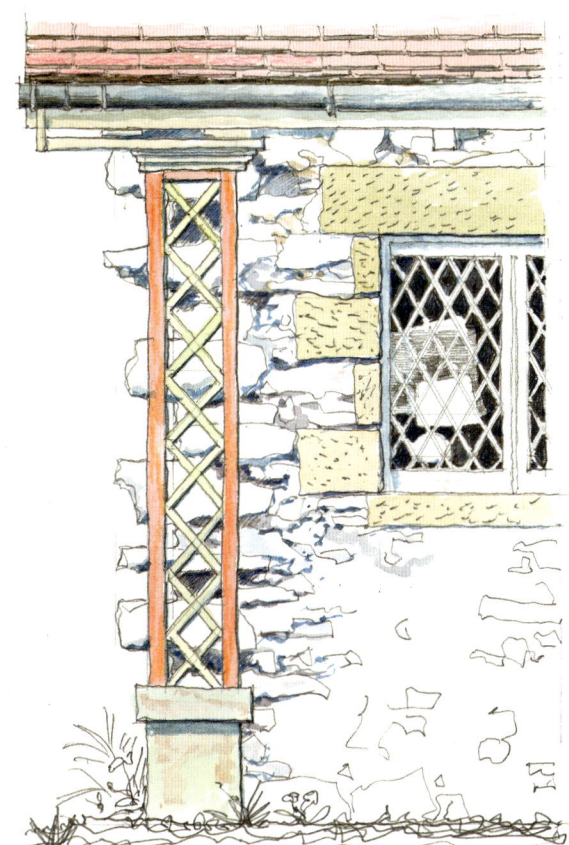

*The Quartz Lodge.*

*Detail of the timber column from Ardimersay Cottage.*

*Window detail.*

*A pair of estate cottages.*

 Over the road, and starkly plain in comparison with the exaggerated textures of the quartz, stands a pair of plain slate-roofed, whitewashed cottages. What makes them unusual for Islay is the use of decorative red ridge tiles and intricately detailed windows.

 The next building along the roadway was built as the Kildalton Post Office. With a pathway leading to its side entrance, it too had plain harled walls but a more exaggerated roof, with decorative timber work supporting overhanging eaves. It looks a little different today, without its original harling, and therefore is closer in character to the two other houses which lie towards the north-eastern edge of the estate grounds. Both are of finely crafted masonry. The larger of the two also has the swept eaves of the quartz house, and a particularly grand chimney.

*Former Kildalton Post Office – a side elevation showing the entrance.*

*A small house dignified by fine craftsmanship.*

*Cnoc Cottages, later known as the Kildalton Dower House.*

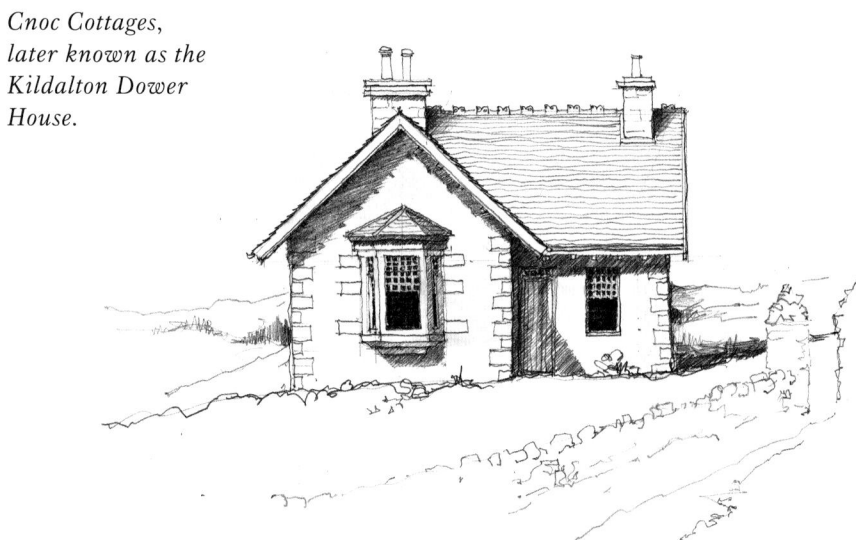

*The north-eastern gatehouse to Kildalton estate.*

To the north-east of the main house, the woodland opens up to a view across a small sandy cove. This is Cnoc Bay. On the rocky promontory overlooking the bay stands what appears to be a much grander building, known as the Dower House. 'Dower House' is a misnomer but gets that name from a later conversion to accommodate the mother of Talbot Clifton, the owner of Kildalton after the Ramsays' departure in the 1920s. In fact, the Dower House began life as purpose-built accommodation for eight separate families (including keepers, ghillies, bailiffs and foresters) skilfully designed to create the appearance of a single imposing dwelling. The two doorways in each of the three porches, and two centrally placed doorways on the seaward façade, show its real purpose. Though less flamboyant, its three-dimensional composition and detailing resemble that of the Castle.

The last of the houses in this sequence stands guard at the gateway on the northern boundary of the Kildalton grounds. Its tight ground-plan and steeply sloping roof accentuate its hilltop location.

*The bathing house on Kilnaughton Bay.*

The Ramsay family also built extensively in and around Port Ellen, including another family residence, Cairnmore House. Perched on the high ground overlooking Kilnaughton Bay to the south of Port Ellen, its woodlands lead down to the shore. On the beach a charming bathing house fashionably masqueraded as a medieval ruin.

John Ramsay died in 1892 and was succeeded by his son Iain. By the 1920s, the distilling industry was a casualty of the general depression, and without adequate income, Kildalton had to be sold. The new owners were Talbot Clifton and his wife Violet. From wealthy landowning families, they shared a passion for adventurous travel. For a man best known for his prowess in stalking and shooting wild animals, the Kildalton estate made an ideal home, and it was here that he was laid to rest in 1928. From his grave on the hillside of Cnoc Rhaonastil (Fairy Hill) the remains of Kildalton Castle can still be glimpsed in the woodlands below.

*Cairnmore House in 1910, after the addition of the conservatory and service wing.*

*In the second major land transaction completed by Charles Morrison of Islay House, Lossit (later Dunlossit) was bought by Sir Smith Child as a sporting estate, but was resold shortly afterwards to Kirkman Finlay and then Donald Martin.*

*Dunlossit estate in 1860.*

*Raised high above the Sound of Islay, Dunlossit Castle remains an awe-inspiring presence.*

# Dunlossit estate

In 1860 Charles Morrison, owner of the Islay House estate, decided to sell off a second swathe of land. Stretching down the Sound of Islay from Port Askaig towards the northern edge of the Kildalton estate, the Lossit (later Dunlossit) estate extended inland as far as the High Road between Port Ellen and Bowmore.

The buyers were the Smith Child family. Sir Smith Child, a banker from Staffordshire, had married the daughter of Major Colin Campbell of Jura and, by 1865, had built a shooting lodge on the clifftop to the south of Port Askaig. This first Dunlossit residence could well have been mistaken for a genuine medieval tower house. Today, it stands tall at the southern end of the main house, where its random rubble stonework sets it apart from the later coursed stonework detailing of the adjoining buildings.

In 1867, only a few years after buying the estate, the Smith Child's eldest son and heir died aged 30, and the estate was sold to Kirkman Finlay, a tea importer from Glasgow. As laird for some 20 years, it was Kirkman Finlay who invested in the much grander version of the Dunlossit house and who planted the surrounding woodlands.

*The first (1865) shooting lodge, sited for dramatic effect and easily mistaken for a genuine medieval fortification.*

The new house of 1874 was designed by Glasgow architect William Spence. He had recently completed an extensive remodelling of Cameron House, on Loch Lomond, to achieve a roofline bristling with decorative turrets and steeply pitched crowstepped gables, transforming it into an accomplished example of the High Victorian Baronial style.

At Dunlossit, the original tower was extended northwards to create a much grander house and southwards to provide ancillary accommodation. The result is even more exuberant than Cameron House, with more turrets, more roughly hewn stone walling, and more intricately carved sandstone detailing. The overall effect, especially when viewed from the water below, would have been carefully conceived so as to evoke an emotional response, one of awe tinged with intrigue.

*The seaward elevation of Dunlossit House with the splayed lower walls of a medieval castle.*

*The landward-facing elevation of Dunlossit House as it looked shortly after remodelling by the Martin family in the early twentieth century.*

Every corner of Dunlossit was adorned with a turret, used because of their association with heroism and nobility. In their original, medieval form, these 'cap-houses' had a serious military purpose, jutting out to form safe vantage points and enclosing stairs onto battlemented roofs.

The Kirkman Finlay house makes up most of today's residence, but the stone porch has been heavily remodelled in more recent times.

In 1890, the Dunlossit estate was sold again, this time to John Ramsay of Kildalton's brother-in-law, Donald Martin. Following a fire which damaged the ground-floor drawing room at the northern end of the building, Dunlossit underwent some interior remodelling. In more recent years, restoration work by the current owners explains the carved monogram (S for Schroder, the merchant banking family who bought the estate in 1937) and the date plaque of MMXII (2012) on the north-easternmost tower.

*Whilst the principal tenant farmers aspired to the grand lifestyle of their lairds, the typical islanders, whose lives had changed little for centuries, lived in dwellings reported to be 'scenes of misery'. Ensuing change in both building and farming practices established the landscape of today.*

1. Finlaggan
2. Cladville
3. Ardnave
4. Kilarrow
5. Kilchiaran
6. Braibruich
7. Ardmore
8. Machrie
9. Uiskentuie
10. Kilnaughton
11. Gartmain
12. Port Ellen

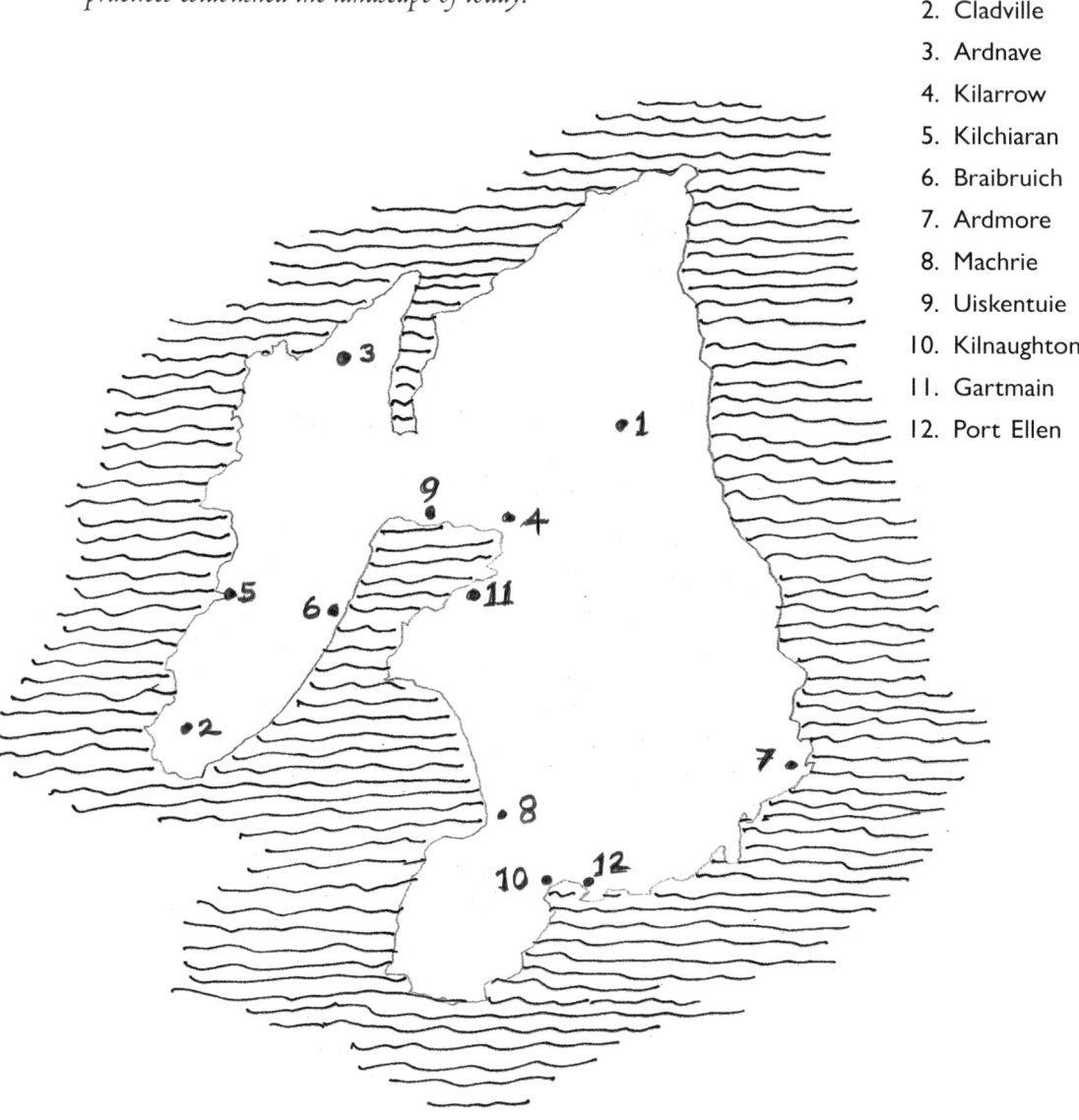

# Farms and steadings

*'... Ila, an ile of twentie mile length from the north to south, and sixteen myle in bredth from the eist to the west, fertil, fruitful, and full of natural grassing.'*

Donald Munro, Dean of the Isles, in his
*Description of the Western Isles of Scotland*, 1563.

# Farmhouses

Neolithic farmers arrived on Islay in around 3800 BC, bringing cereal crops and domesticated animals with them. Barley and oats were to prove well-suited to the terrain, as were cattle, sheep and pigs. Not only did the fertility of the arable land and the quality of grazing support steady population growth, but the abundance, in comparison to neighbouring islands, made Islay a territory worth fighting for.

More recent agricultural activity has mostly erased any traces of how people lived or how the landscape was used to feed the military might of the Norse invaders and the ensuing Clan Donald dynasty. However, there is longstanding evidence that islanders sought the relative security offered by the natural and manmade islets of inland lochs. The most significant of these, in Loch Finlaggan, was to become the chief meeting place for the leadership of the MacDonald Lords of the Isles.

In its heyday Finlaggan boasted a Council Chamber, Great Hall, chapel and residence, a place of power-broking, spiritual guidance and feasting. When the MacDonalds lost control of Islay towards the end of the fifteenth century, the buildings of Finlaggan, long invested with a significance beyond their physical presence, were dismantled.

Today, a sixteenth-century farmhouse stands amid the ruins, apparently the home of Donald MacGillespie. Named as leaseholder of the lands around Finlaggan at the time, his resplendent stone effigy lies nearby. Fashioned from the ruins of the former feasting hall, the tall, straight, lime-mortared masonry walls and detailing in imported sandstone would have set this residence firmly apart from the more typical field-stone and turf houses of the farming community clustered around it.

The way in which this community cultivated the land remains clearly legible. Any unbuilt areas have been shaped by digging parallel trenches and using the earth to raise the ground between them. These raised beds would have been fertilised with seaweed ready for planting.

Although itself unfortified, the island location and sturdy construction of MacGillespie's house would have afforded considerable security as inter-clan skirmishes rumbled on. A contemporary sixteenth-century map drawn by Timothy Pont indicates a number of sizeable residences scattered across Islay, but the Finlaggan example is an exceptional survivor. It alone gives us some idea about those who played a part in determining land use around this time. Other examples were seemingly either casualties of sustained feuding or built over at a later date.

*Donald MacGillespie's ruined sixteenth-century farmhouse in Loch Finlaggan, fashioned from the former feasting hall of the MacDonald Lords of the Isles.*

Records from the early years of the seventeenth century describe how the lands of Islay, by then part of the kingdom of Scotland, were managed by the new owners, the Campbells of Cawdor. A superior class of principal tenants known as 'tacksmen' were granted the rights to control considerable swathes of land, typically overseeing a two-tier system of subtenants and labourers. Tacksmen lived in expectation that their rights were hereditary and typically took on the name of their principal seat. Most were relatives of the Cawdor Campbell landowners, a sensible precaution whilst uprisings remained a threat. This reliance on kin was rooted in the former clan system, where allegiance had been essential to retaining power.

An additional and unusual arrangement, particularly favoured by the Cawdor Campbell lairds, involved granting land rights to some of their principal tenants in return for lump sum down payments. These one-off payments, known as 'wadsets', meant that the tenant was no longer required to pay rent and could enjoy continuity of tenure until such time as his wadset was repaid in full. For the laird this system created an immediate and welcome source of capital. For the wadsetters it offered complete freedom to determine land use, and to benefit from all of the monies generated.

Little, if any, income trickled upwards to the laird. By the beginning of the eighteenth century the Campbells of Cawdor, who had hoped to prosper when they claimed the island a century earlier, were facing financial ruin and were forced to sell their lands to the Campbells of Shawfield.

The first of the Shawfield lairds, the 'Great' Daniel Campbell, recognised that the inherited tenancy system lacked the incentive required for his planned agricultural improvements. Accordingly, although it was not realised under his lairdship, he set in train a process of land reformation. A set of maps, drawn up by the surveyor Stephen MacDougall for the incoming laird, recorded a number of large 'mansions', seemingly the homes of tacksmen, whose wealth is evident from their possessions, listed as fine furniture, silverware, feather beds and so on. Anxious about Daniel's proposed changes to their tenure, some of the wealthiest tacksmen chose to emigrate. Those who stayed on sought to follow their laird's example, looking to increase their productivity.

*The original early Georgian farmhouse at Cladville, typical of the comparatively grand and fashionable homes built by the wealthier principal tenants (tacksmen).*

On the south-west tip of Islay the success of one Islay tacksman is particularly evident. At Cladville, the original house still stands next to its more opulent early nineteenth-century extension. The original Cladville looks to date from the early years of the eighteenth century. The builder was probably Lauchlan Campbell, a tacksman of Cawdor Campbell kin.

Although much smaller than the contemporary Islay House, Cladville embodied the same Georgian fashion for creating a tastefully refined façade. Symmetrical, smoothly finished and carefully proportioned, the front elevation differed markedly from the small-windowed irregularity of its purely functional back elevation. Despite the modest size of his home, the inventory at the time of Lauchlan Campbell's death in 1737 shows it to have been a well-furnished home, with tables, chairs, chests, presses and a goodly range of pewter tableware.

*Cladville's late Georgian central bay stands between the original house (with porch) and dairy.*

    Even this first house would have been impressive in comparison to the typical islanders' homes which had changed little since the sixteenth century. And, whilst the siting of Cladville can be understood in terms of practical considerations such as ground conditions, southerly aspect, natural shelter and fresh water from a nearby well, its hillside positioning and dominance over the landscape would undoubtedly have enhanced the status of its occupants.

    From the comparative scale, ceiling heights and window-size of the later Georgian styled extension at Cladville, it is evident that the new farming practices were proving satisfyingly lucrative.

*Ardnave House and farm steading in around 1780.*

At Ardnave, on the north-western tip of the island, this process of aggrandisement is also evident. Duncan Campbell, whose grave of 1825 commands the high ground overlooking Nave Island, inherited control over several farms, a number of dwellings and a mill, when his father John died in 1765. It is likely that the home Duncan inherited was the two-storied rectangular stone building (very similar to the early house at Cladville) which forms the core of the current Ardnave House. This original house was probably built in the 1740s after the Campbells took on the lease, as the previous leaseholder's main residence had been on the other side of Loch Gruinart at Killinallan.

Under Duncan's tenure, the Campbells of Ardnave amassed wealth and status. One of his daughters, Jane, married Captain Archibald MacDonald, who was buried in the same grave as his father-in-law and left an estate of considerable value. Jane's sister Barbara married the Count of Polignac, who had family ties to Prince Rainier of Monaco.

Duncan Campbell transformed Ardnave by creating a tall-ceilinged bow-fronted first-floor drawing room above an entry parlour to the front of the house. To the rear, he added a grand first-floor dining room served by a ground-floor kitchen and dairy. The roof timbers were fixed with pegs fashioned from sharpened heather, an ingenious use of local materials.

The effect of Duncan's works to the house at Ardnave would have been suitably impressive, but was further enhanced by the fanciful dairy built

*The tacksman's house at Ardnave with the additional bow-fronted upper parlour.*

*The Ardnave dairy façade as it might have looked painted with trompe l'œil windows in the manner of the Inverary example.*

alongside. Whilst unique on Islay, it is similar to one dating from the 1750s in Tombreac, Inveraray. Designed by John Adam for the Duke of Argyll, the Inverary version was built as a polite façade to mask the workings of the farmyard behind, and its illusion of grandeur was enhanced by plasterwork painted to look as if the blank openings held real windows. At Tombreac, the *trompe l'œil* windows matched those in the turrets of the Castle. The fact that both the size and shape of the Ardnave recesses are also a match for the Inveraray Castle windows suggests that Tombreac was indeed the model for this Islay indulgence.

*'A set of people worn down with poverty; their habitations scenes of misery, made of loose stones; without chimnies, without doors, excepting the faggot opposed to the wind at one or other of the appertures permitting the smoke to escape through the other, in order to prevent suffocation. The furniture perfectly corresponds; a pothook hangs from the middle of the roof, with a pot pendant over a grateless fire, filled with fare that may rather be called a permission to exist, than a support of vigorous life; the inmates, as may be expected, lean, withered, dusky and smoke dried.'*

Thomas Pennant, 1772

In stark contrast to the relatively grand lifestyle enjoyed by Islay's tacksmen, the experience of life for the majority of the island population was very different. During his short visit to Islay in 1772, the observant visitor Thomas Pennant accompanied one of his hosts, the Campbell laird of Ballinaby, on an expedition to the caves at the north-western tip of the island. They passed by many typical rural homes on the way, and Pennant's account of life within one such remains the most vivid description of wretched existence.

These homes are long gone, but their traces across the island bear witness to the efforts of generation upon generation to cultivate even seemingly barren land. Imprints that look to have been made by a giant comb surround the raised stone and turf footprints of houses once crafted from the landscape.

The eighteenth-century examples witnessed by Pennant had changed little for over 200 years. Remains from the sixteenth century are similar in form and scale, though more ovoid than rectangular in plan. Some of the earliest seem to have been basket-like in construction, with interwoven slender timber branches wrapped in a thick outer layer of turf and heather thatch. Others had walls of rough field stones, a weightier construction that would have been able to support more substantial roof frames made from pairs of inclined timbers with a long ridge beam. On Islay, suitable timber was unusually scarce. As the native trees were few and slight, even driftwood was a valuable resource, and admonishments from landowners suggest that islanders often removed their precious structural framing timbers for reuse when moving home.

Smoke from burning peat rose from a central hearth on the earthen floor and dried peat was also used as insulation, filling the cavity between an inner and an outer layer of stone walling. Without the fine timber or glass needed to craft doors and windows, openings were small, few and carefully positioned to vent the smoke. Thatched roofs were refreshed in summer months, with a mixture of heather, reeds, ferns and straw.

By the end of the eighteenth century, new, imported ways of building were becoming more widespread. Another acclaimed naturalist and explorer, Joseph Banks, visited Islay a month before Pennant, accompanied by a group of artists who recorded buildings, landscape and wildlife. The images from Banks' visit were then used to illustrate Pennant's account, and it is these illustrations which reveal signs of a transition from old ways to new practices. Whilst recording the ruins at Kilarrow, Banks was intrigued by the nearby home of a weaver and instructed the artist John Frederick Miller to make a set of drawings of it. Although similar in many ways to the example described by Pennant, the weaver's cottage drawings show refinements such as openings framed in timber and windows filled with small rectangular panes of glass.

*Weaver's cottage: south (facing Loch Indaal) and east elevations.*

*Weaver's cottage: north (facing Kilarrow) and west elevations, based on information recorded by John Frederick Miller.*

*A thatched cottage still inhabited by a crofter and his family in the early twentieth century.*

Other illustrations from the same visit show houses built by the wealthy merchants of Kilarrow. These were of more regular, quarried stone and the taller, straighter walls supported wider roof spans. Some were two-storied, all had chimneys built into their gable walls and all had glazed widows. Even greater change is evident in a distant sketch of a fledgling Bowmore, where the handful of new houses already stood even taller than those of Kilarrow, with more generous windows, slated roofs and walls smoothed over with lime-washed harling, in the style of Islay House.

Pennant may have been troubled by the disparity between opulence and poverty, but not surprised. Living conditions on Islay accorded with those he had observed across the Highlands and Islands. Indeed, the endurance of the same basic house-type says a lot about the ingenuity involved in making such effective use of such scanty materials. Some were still in use well into the twentieth century.

Transformation of building practice and land settlement on Islay was relatively slow and patchy in comparison to other parts of Scotland. The process began with the early eighteenth-century commissioning of Stephen MacDougall's maps. These not only recorded the existing situation so as to establish farm boundaries, but were also used to propose improvements in land usage.

Subsequent rental records for each of these holdings tracked the nature and pace of change. By the start of the nineteenth century, most wadsetters' loans had been repaid, their lands repossessed by the laird and then reallocated. Some holdings were consolidated under single tenants. Others were shared between a number of families, each paying rent directly to the laird. Others again, typically in remote less fertile areas, continued the clan-based farming traditions. In clustered townships or 'townlands', families subsisted by cultivating small plots and sharing grazing rights.

This variety in land settlement on Islay resulted in a number of different building types. The single tenants of larger farms aspired to the lifestyle of their lairds and major leaseholders, so built accordingly with an eye on style. Initially, this meant echoing the Georgian aesthetic, but this was gradually displaced by the more complex forms and exposed stonework of the Victorian period.

On farms with multiple tenants, the new lease agreements required each family to construct drains, field walls and buildings to meet set standards. Houses were to be of quarried stone set in lime mortar, with slated roofs. Typically single-storied, some with rooms in the roof space, their central doorway was flanked by two vertical sash windows, and gable-end chimneys vented the hearths.

On the shared townlands, families continued to build their traditional low-lying, thick-walled, thatch-roofed cottages.

*This cross-sectional drawing shows the construction and interior of a crofter's cottage that was still occupied in the twentieth century, based on photographs in the Museum of Islay Life's collection. The museum also displays many of the items illustrated, including box beds.*

*'What will you see or hear in these fertile townlands, where the hum of busy farmers used to be heard, with the rattling of carts, ploughs and harrows in spring, and the songs of the reapers in harvest, and the social gatherings of youths in winter? Nothing but sheep pens, and two or three shepherds' houses, and there is nothing to break the deathlike silence that prevails everywhere but the whistle of the shepherd, the barking of his dogs, and the bleating of sheep! Fertile townlands throughout the island in the same condition. Sheep-farming may pay the farmer and the laird for a time; but it will never promote the prosperity of a place like Islay, where so much of the land is arable.'*

Archibald Sinclair, quoted in *The Kilchoman People Vindicated*, The Islay Association, 28 June 1867.

During the first 50 years of the Shawfield Campbell lairdship, the population of Islay had almost doubled. In part this was due to an increase in alternative employment, in part to inoculation against childhood disease and in part to more productive land usage. The new crops and farming methods resulted in better yields. Even small acreages were proving viable. The newly introduced potatoes thrived and quickly became a significant part of the diet. On the joint-tenancy farms and remaining traditional townlands, families expanded and new houses sprung up amongst the old. At the time, the island economy looked to be sustainable, and population growth was generally regarded as a sign of progress. Sadly, this optimism was to be short lived.

Only a few years into the new century, changes in circumstance began to take their toll. The export prices for Islay's produce, which had benefitted from the trading embargoes of the Napoleonic wars, plummeted following the declaration of peace in 1815. That same year brought exceptionally inclement weather and a meagre harvest. Similar adverse weather events were to devastate crops periodically over the next 20 years. Then, in 1845, the first potato blight arrived from Ireland.

In the meantime, the population had continued to grow. By the 1840s it had trebled since the first years of the Shawfield Campbells, from 5,000 to 15,000.

*One of the many abandoned mid-nineteenth-century houses amidst earlier ruins. This is a typical example, built by one branch of a family who were joint tenants on a single farm. Its form and construction accord with the standards required by the laird in order to secure the lease.*

Between 1845 and 1848, many islanders were forced to emigrate. Not only were they facing starvation, but their leases were terminated as the Shawfield Campbell's bankruptcy brought their tenure to an abrupt end. Across the island, the clustered farming settlements of the joint tenancies and townlands were abandoned.

Addressing the Glasgow-based Islay Association some 20 years after the famine years, Archibald Sinclair, who had been born in a small Islay holding, shared between 12 farmers, spoke of the deep sadness felt by the many who had had no choice but to leave.

*'Not only cleanly in their personal and domestic habits but decidedly more so than could be expected from the external appearance of many of their dwellings, and such as had no bothy or byre attached for their cattle were, consequently, obliged to have them stalled in the lower end of the house; but partitioned off by placing a couple of close timber beds across the house, with the backs to the cattle, having a door of entrance betwixt, the upper ending in one or two apartments warm and comfortable for the habitation of a working man and family – free from all disagreeable smell, except occasionally that of the peat reek ...'*

Duncan Campbell of Ellister, quoted in
*The Kilchoman People Vindicated.*

## Farm steadings

For most of those who worked the land it was perfectly normal to live under one roof alongside their livestock, sometimes with little subdivision, and many did so until the late 1800s. By contrast, the animals of Islay House had, since around 1780, enjoyed purpose-built accommodation, an example emulated by the other landowners and principal tenants.

The most extraordinary of these grand farm steadings dates from 1826. On the west coast at Kilchiaran, Walter Frederick Campbell, the last of the Shawfield lairds, invested in a range of buildings for an incoming tenant. What he built was unprecedented and remarkable. Alongside a relatively modest farmhouse, he commissioned a steading that sought to be as elegant as it was functional.

The natural amphitheatre of its valley location is approached from all landward directions through the heights of the surrounding hills, ideal vantage points from which to appreciate the perfect semicircle of Kilchiaran and the symmetry of its radiating subdivision.

Although unique on Islay, the Kilchiaran steading shows a striking resemblance to the building and landscape at Maam, Glenshira, near Inveraray. In 1785 this had been designed by Robert Mylne for the Duke of Argyll. The intention at Maam was to build a full circle of buildings. Only half was ever completed.

Clearly Kilchiaran was built to impress, but at considerable cost. Not only was this a lavishly expensive building project, but it must also have caused Walter Frederick some unease. This was a laird noted for his stance against eviction and yet at Kilchiaran he did just that. Seventeen families were relocated, mostly to newly constructed villages.

*Kilchiaran steading on Islay's west coast included a shed for four carts, stables, byre, milking parlour and a water-powered threshing machine.*

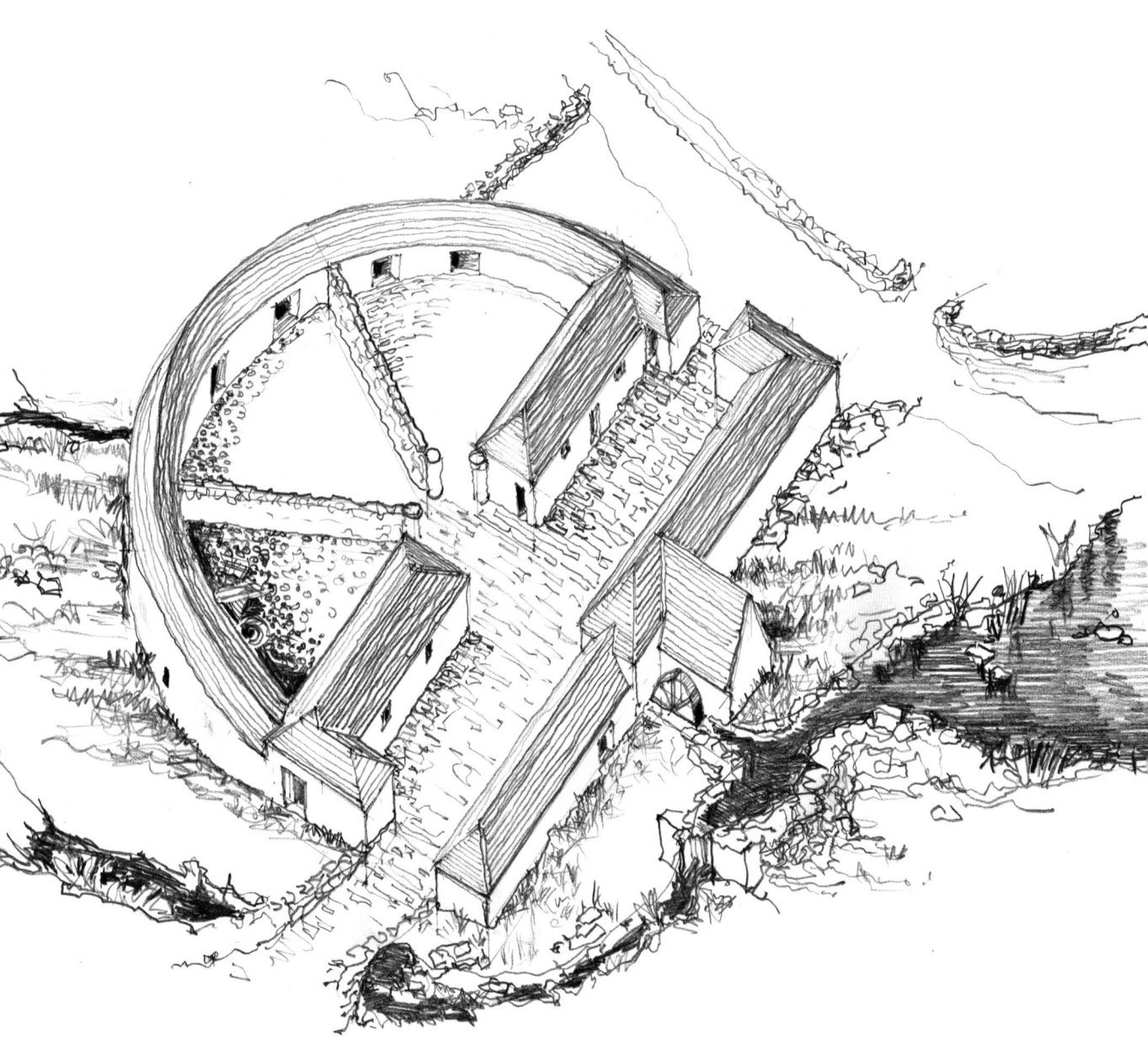

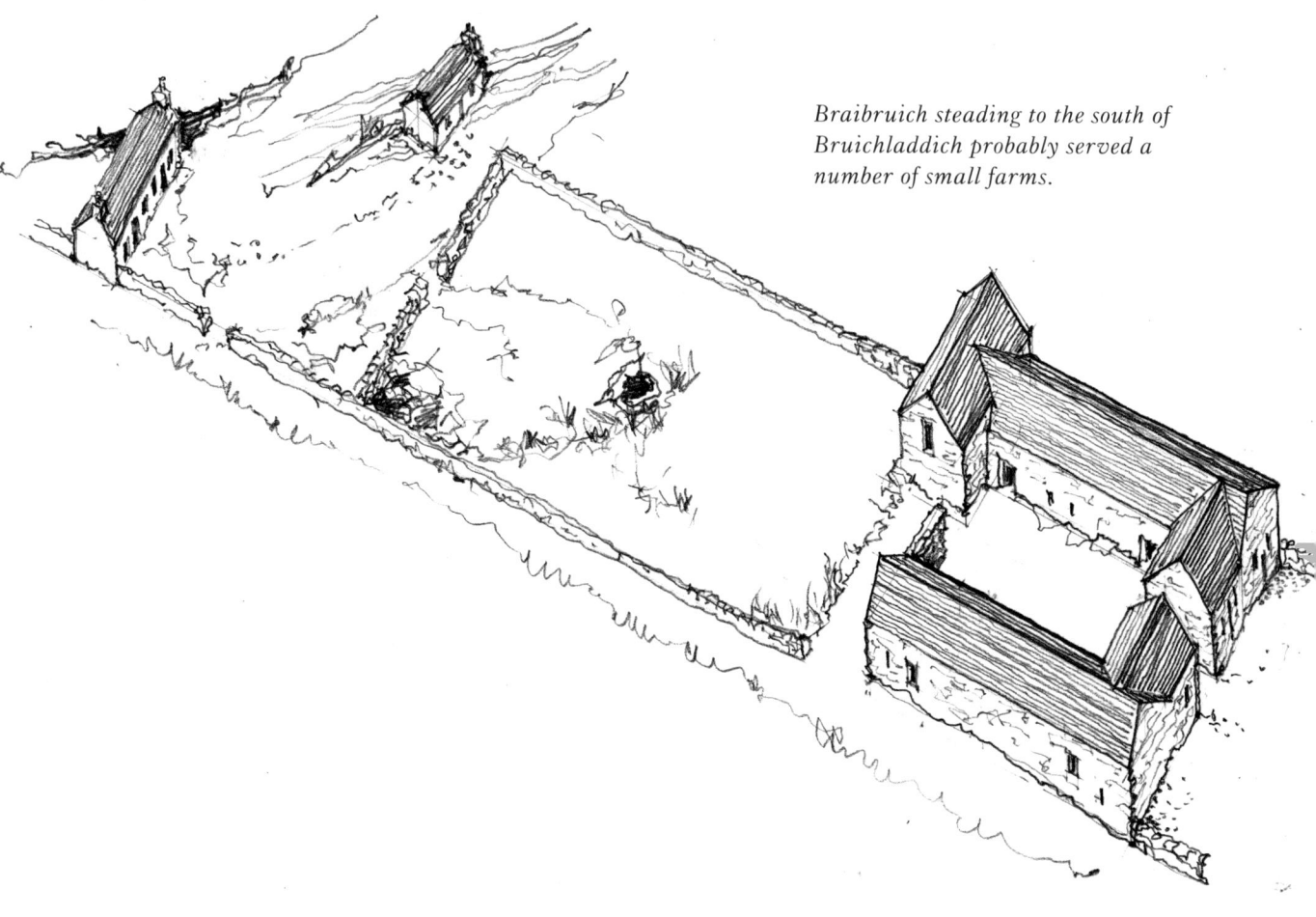

*Braibruich steading to the south of Bruichladdich probably served a number of small farms.*

Elsewhere on the island there are other examples of generous buildings constructed to house cattle and horses. Typically these date from the latter part of the 1800s, when export markets started to recover from the mid-century slump. The upturn in the markets, especially for cattle, saw renewed investment, and at Braibruich, to the south of Bruichladdich, an impressive steading dwarfed the farmer's cottages that stood behind it.

In the 50 years since the devastating famine of the 1840s, the pattern of tenure had changed dramatically. Most of the traditional clustered farming settlements had been replaced by single tenants on larger, more viable acreages, and the majority of today's farmhouses and steadings were either built or renovated in Victorian times.

On the eastern side of the island, the laird John Ramsay had long taken an active interest in the potential for agricultural improvement. He sought to encourage change by example, very much in the manner of the Shawfield Campbells. After buying the extensive Kildalton estate in the late 1850s, he set about building a substantial number of two-storied farmhouses, each abutted by byres, stables, barns and dairies, to enclose a generous courtyard.

Many continued as working farms, whilst others, such as Ardmore House, were restored to serve new estates created in the twentieth century. Ardmore, now home to the Mactaggart family lairds of the north-eastern part of the Kildalton estate, had a similar history to that of Ardnave. Home to a wealthy Campbell tacksman in the early eighteenth century, the original Georgian house was probably incorporated into John Ramsay's nineteenth-century farmhouse and steading.

*A typical farm and steading, including barn, byre, stable, cart shed and milking parlour, from the latter part of the 1800s, one of many built on the Kildalton estate by the laird John Ramsay.*

In 1891 John Ramsay also played a major part in converting another example, the Machrie Farm, into a guesthouse and golf club. The initial proposal came from whisky entrepreneur Peter Mackie. Like the much older John Ramsay, Peter came from a Stirlingshire family with interests in distilling, arrived on Islay as a young man and quickly enjoyed considerable success at Lagavulin.

On the Machrie Farm, sand blown inland from the 7-mile-long Laggan Bay overlaid a peaty hinterland to support the finest quality of turf, dotted with sand dunes. Traditionally these coastal grasslands, 'machair' in Gaelic, provided grazing and patches of cultivation, but a young golf professional from Musselburgh, Willie Campbell, saw another potential use. Working with nature, he created the fine new golf course which opened in 1891.

By 1910, another four golf courses had been established, one on Uiskentuie farmland at the head of Loch Indaal, one (very briefly) at Kilnaughton Bay, one between Bowmore and Ballygrant at Gartmain, and one behind the Ramsay Hall in Port Ellen. Only the Machrie course continued to flourish.

*Originally the home of a wealthy seventeenth-century tacksman, Ardmore House was rebuilt in the nineteenth century.*

*Converted from a typical Ramsay farm and steading, Machrie House opened to guests in 1892 and, as part of the Machrie Hotel, continues to provide a characterful core to the internationally acclaimed golf venue.*

During the latter half of the nineteenth century, several factors contributed to a rapid transformation of land usage across the island. In addition to golf courses, grazing for sheep and peat-cutting to feed the distilleries, the cultivation of less fertile uplands gave way to deer, pheasant and grouse.

Throughout these and subsequent changing circumstances, Islay's farming community was to prove resilient, adapting to new markets and looking to continue the long tradition of 'improvement' initiated by the 'Great' Daniel Campbell. One measure of success has been the island's continuing reputation for rearing fine quality stock, a reputation undoubtedly promoted by the Islay, Jura and Colonsay Agricultural Association, formed in 1838 and still serving its purpose today.

*Built by islanders enticed from rural traditions by new opportunities, these were the most crucial part of the landowners' grand designs for radical social, economic and scenic transformation.*

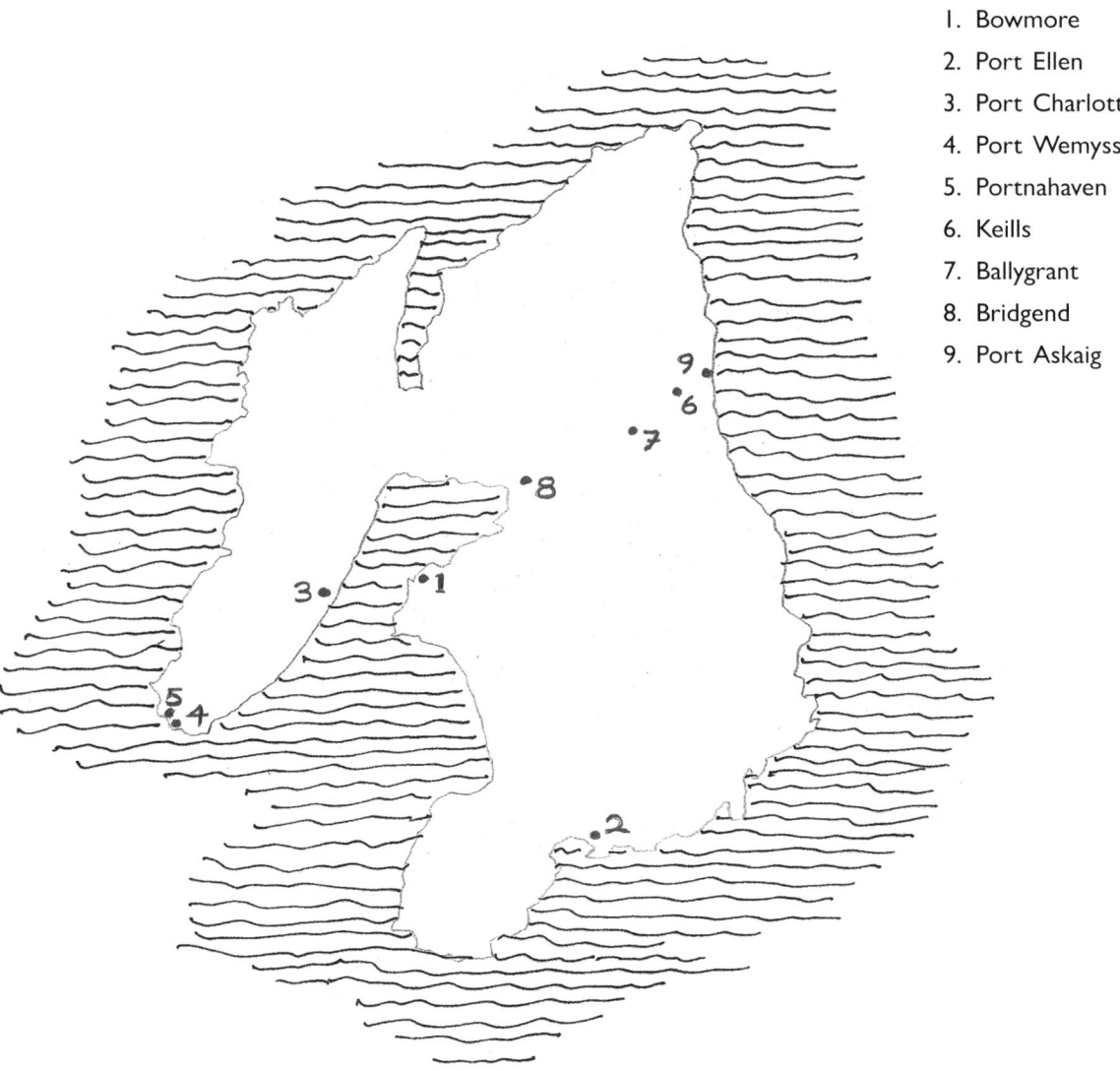

1. Bowmore
2. Port Ellen
3. Port Charlotte
4. Port Wemyss
5. Portnahaven
6. Keills
7. Ballygrant
8. Bridgend
9. Port Askaig

# Villages

# A village house

*Whether one- or two-storied, each rigorously symmetrical front façade had to be like its neighbour. Rubble stone walls were coated with harling and lime-washed to achieve a smooth white finish. Window openings edged with sandstone, similar in size, glazing type and Palladian in proportion, were evenly spaced around a double-leafed front door.*

*No finesse was required for the rear of the houses. Non-aligned smaller widows were built into exposed rubble walls, entirely of local stone.*

*Uniform façades line public spaces in Port Charlotte. A survey of 1878 shows the corner house, with archway, to be the village inn shortly before the construction of Dick's (now Port Charlotte) Hotel.*

*Buildings for livestock and workshops behind the façades.*

## Bowmore

The building of Bowmore was recorded in 1772 by John Cleveley, one of the artists accompanying the visiting naturalist Sir Joseph Banks. In Cleveley's view (drawn from the head of Loch Indaal) the church is newly completed, a line of thatched cottages curve along the shore towards the new town, a few warehouses and fishermen's stores cluster around the quay and the first of the smooth-walled, slate-roofed houses stand nearby.

At the same time as this, work on Edinburgh New Town had barely started and the construction of Inverary was yet to begin, placing Bowmore firmly in the vanguard of the Scottish New Town movement. Based on the same ideas that underpin Georgian planning whatever the scale, the carefully proportioned houses of Bowmore formed terraces to line public spaces, each sized to suit its purpose. Significant institutions were strategically positioned as focal points, whilst more utilitarian activities lay out of sight behind the façades.

Unsurprisingly, given the friendship between the Shawfield Campbells and the Dukes of Argyll, some aspects of Bowmore are similar to Inveraray. In both cases the main street leads from quay to church and, in William Adam's initial plan for Inverary, a round church was also the focal point.

In Bowmore the generous Main Street was designed to accommodate the island's markets and fairs. Even with today's traffic, it can be understood as a grand communal 'room with a view'. The rising slope up to the round church acts as the visual enclosure to a space which affords sweeping views across the loch.

Following the death of his grandfather, Daniel Campbell the Younger had assumed responsibility for this major project, and it was he who controlled the outcome, dictating plot size, overall form, building materials

*The quayside warehouses, the freshly built church and one of the new houses, drawn here based on information recorded by John Cleveley in 1772.*

*The same view in 1830, based on William Heath's painting, one of a series commissioned by Walter Frederick Campbell.*

and elevational composition to achieve the desired uniformity. He did not, however, fund the construction. Houses were individually built by each family, so varied slightly in scale and detail. Edicts, such as 'all roofs to be slated', could not be insisted upon, and some remained thatched well into the twentieth century.

Whilst the façades mimicked those of the island's wealthier tenants, merchants and clergy, the Bowmore houses were typically occupied by several generations of one family or shared by two or more families. Water came from wells sunk behind the houses. Peats, cut in the summer months, were stacked in time for winter, and fish or seal oil fuelled the lamps.

Some brought their trades with them, others came from crofting settlements and, to enable continued self-sufficiency, were entitled to access small acreages around the village. As well as cultivating oats, barley and potatoes, villagers built behind their homes to accommodate dairy cattle, pigs and poultry. Some had a horse and cart.

One of the reasons for relocating commercial activity from Kilarrow was to access the navigable quay developed on the Bowmore site in the 1750s. In the 1790s, a new pier encouraged the development of trade, specifically that of the shoreside distillery. Located at the foot of the hillside and made from the same materials as the village and church, the distillery buildings have long contributed to the scenic character of the village.

The distillery was to play a key role in ensuring long-term viability for the new community. In addition to providing employment, the supply of 'draff', the malted barley solids left over from the distilling process, provided a valuable winter feed for the village livestock.

Some 20 years after the Cleveley drawing, Bowmore had over 100 new houses and 500 inhabitants, and in 1830, the artist William Heath recorded the bustling street scene of a Bowmore fair day.

*Port Ellen in 1900 with the Georgian terraces curving around the bay from the fishermen's cottages and St John's church in the foreground, to the Steamer tavern and the Victorian police station on the shore side, and the Victorian Pier Road buildings beyond.*

# Port Ellen

Islay was to undergo the most significant contributions to its scenic and architectural heritage under the direction of Walter Frederick Campbell, the 4th Shawfield laird, and his uncle Captain Walter Campbell, laird of the Sunderland estate. Foremost amongst the developments from this era were the villages of Port Ellen, Port Charlotte, Port Wemyss and Portnahaven. All were designed to develop and further diversify opportunities for employment.

Founded in the 1820s, Port Ellen was named after Walter Frederick's wife Ellinor and sited to take advantage of the naturally sheltered Leodamus Bay. Plans to attract the herring fleet and commercial fishing proved overly optimistic, but the village thrived along with the distilling industry which developed at nearby Ardbeg, Lagavulin and Laphroaig, as well as in Port Ellen itself.

A survey dated 1852, by Lieutenant J. Ward RN, shows the horseshoe of Frederick Crescent's terraced houses opening directly onto the beach, and further terraces extending along the two newly built roadways, one to Bowmore, the other towards Laphroaig. The uniformity of Port Ellen's houses was due in part to the fact that only those with two-storied houses were entitled to vote. As in Bowmore, homes came with grazing rights, and many built byres and stables for their animals.

In 1832, deeply affected by the loss of his wife, Ellinor, Walter Frederick created a memorial that was not only timelessly handsome but also performed a role of critical importance, Carraig Fhada lighthouse. The architect, David Hamilton, was no lighthouse engineer, but he was well qualified to create an evocative monument. He came from a family of stonemasons, and in addition to authoring grand classical style masterpieces such as Glasgow's Royal Exchange (now the Gallery of Modern Art), his practice left a legacy of finely sculpted memorials, such as that to Nelson on Glasgow Green.

From the earliest days of Port Ellen, local merchants sailed schooners from the wharf, but the building of a stone pier in 1847 enabled access for paddle-steamers. The first of a series named 'Islay' served the distilleries and carried the island's mail. At least one 'Islay' still lies beneath the waves at the treacherous mouth of Port Ellen Bay. The improved harbour also stimulated a tourist industry. By 1850 the Steamer Tavern had opened on the shore, opposite the end of the roadway to Bowmore which also boasted a much grander hotel, the White Hart (now No 1 Charlotte Street).

When the laird John Ramsay died in 1892, his son Iain commissioned a Community Hall as a memorial to his father. The architect, Sydney Mitchell, had also designed the new parish church of St John's. Both buildings stand apart from the uniform terraced houses, the church to the east, the hall to the west. Both differ from and complement the simpler forms of their neighbours.

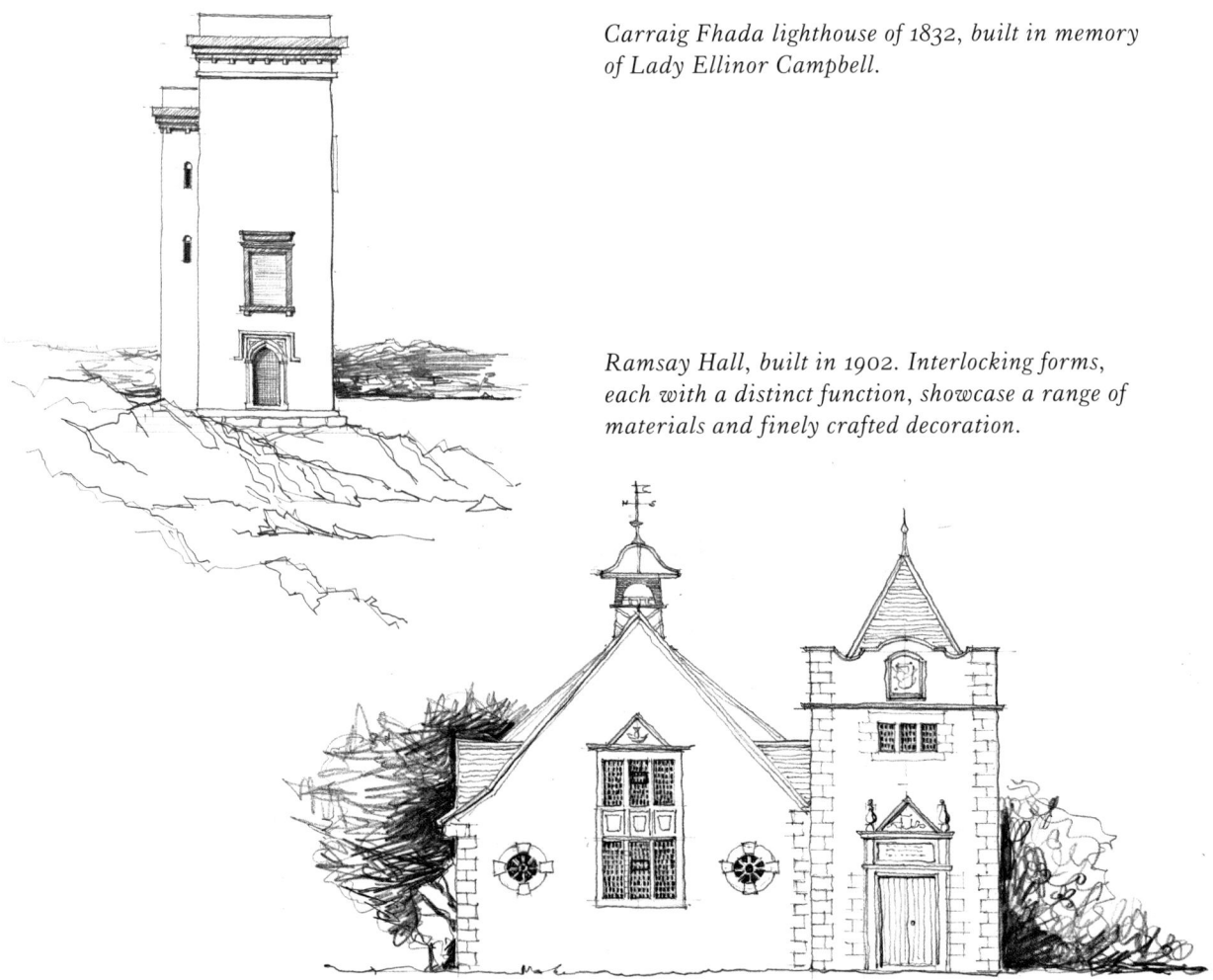

*Carraig Fhada lighthouse of 1832, built in memory of Lady Ellinor Campbell.*

*Ramsay Hall, built in 1902. Interlocking forms, each with a distinct function, showcase a range of materials and finely crafted decoration.*

*Lorgbaw House on the banks of the Gearach Burn sited next to the ferry and inn which predated the building of Port Charlotte.*

# Port Charlotte

On the other side of the island, the village of Port Charlotte was founded in 1828. Named after Walter Frederick's mother, Lady Charlotte Campbell (daughter of the 5th Duke of Argyll), Port Charlotte faces Bowmore across Loch Indaal. Lying on the coastal route around the shores of the Loch, its headland had already made it the ideal place for a ferry crossing from Sgioba (to the north of the Gearach Burn) to Gartbreck (to the south of Bowmore).

Nearly a century before the founding of the new village, Sgioba was already the site of a thriving inn, or 'change-house', providing travellers with fresh horses, serving beer (and probably whisky) from a mill and malt kiln. The wealth of the area's principal tenant, or 'tacksman', is evident from

*By 1900, new shoreside warehousing and the original Lochindaal distillery framed the entrance to Port Charlotte across the Gearach Burn.*

*The former Port Charlotte school, adapted from the abandoned Established Church which had been built in 1830, forms the main focal point of the village.*

the grand, multi-chimneyed Lorgbaw House, that stands on the north side of the Gearach Burn. Similar in concept to Bowmore, Port Charlotte's Georgian grid overlaid an undulating landscape, creating gracefully curved terraces which echo the profile of the coastline. As at Bowmore, a central spine rose steeply from shore to a hilltop church. Here, a plainer, rectangular church was placed squarely to close the vista. Unfortunately, completion of the church coincided with a fundamental shift away from the established religion, and the villagers decided to build their own Free Church (now the Museum of Islay Life). The intended church became the school.

Port Charlotte's main attraction was employment in the Lochindaal distillery, founded in 1832. Built on the banks of the Gearach as it reached the shore, whisky barrels were floated out to waiting boats and the river provided power as well as water for distilling. The distillery dictated the rhythm of life. Production ceased during the driest summer months, allowing time for cleaning and maintenance. Buildings were freshly lime-washed, a practice which extended to the regular repainting of the village houses.

The building of Port Charlotte came at a critical time for the island. Up to this point there had been an optimism about the potential for improving agricultural output, but as the rural population grew, market values for produce fell and harvests failed. Prospects looked increasingly bleak and many were tempted from their land by work opportunities and reassurances about rights to graze and cultivate designated lands around the village. Initially the plan succeeded, but with much reduced acreage at their disposal and the eventual demise of Lochindaal distillery in the depression of the early twentieth century, many looked back on their more independent crofting lives with some regret.

By the mid-twentieth century little remained of Port Charlotte's distillery, but vestiges of village life survived: the regular daily processions of dairy cattle to and from milking, the sharing of fish as locally crafted wooden boats were hauled ashore, and the butcher's shop masked within a square of façades. This was a rhythm of life born of a desire to sustain a village community.

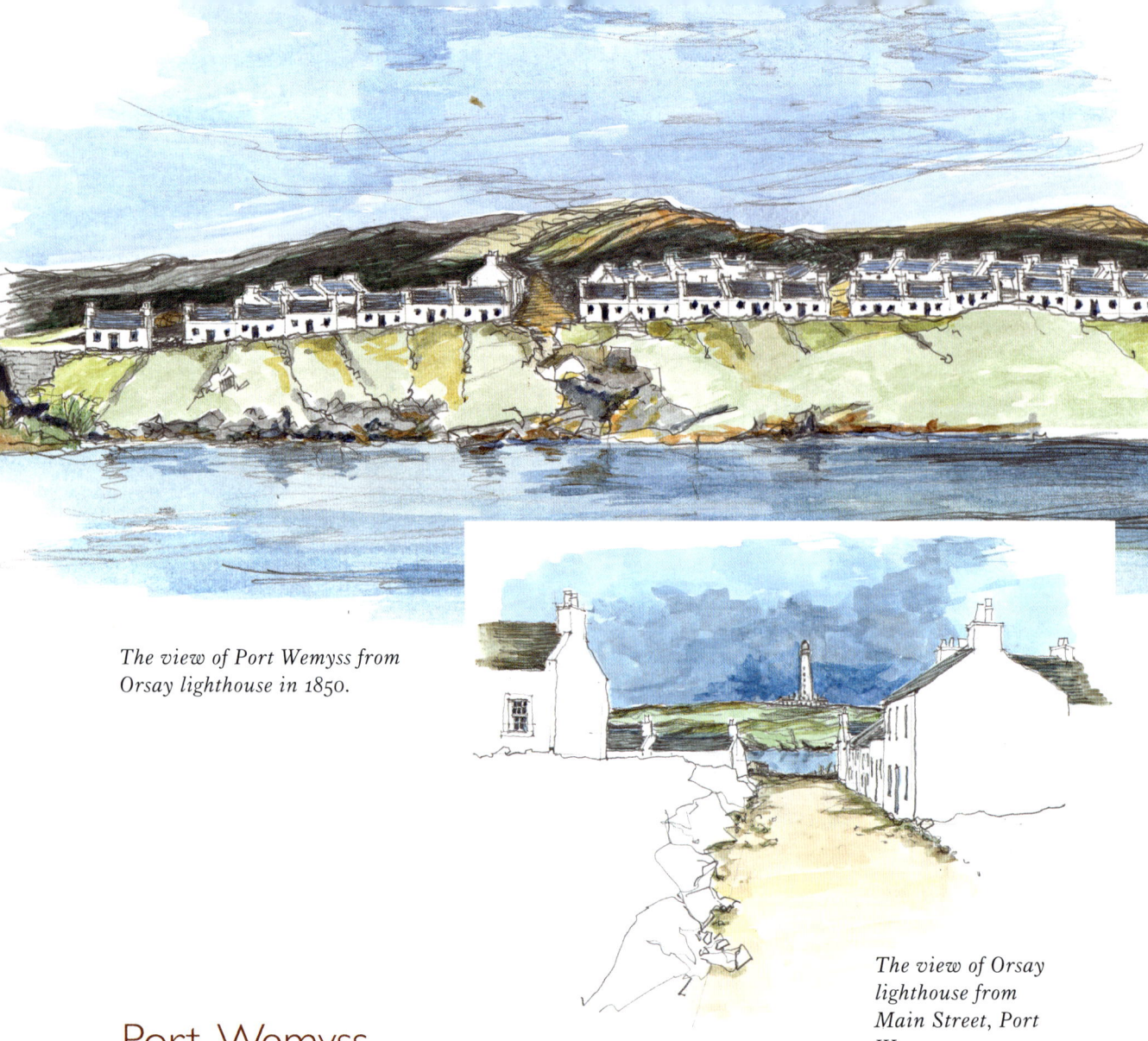

*The view of Port Wemyss from Orsay lighthouse in 1850.*

*The view of Orsay lighthouse from Main Street, Port Wemyss.*

# Port Wemyss

The lochside roadway was extended to the southernmost tip of the Rhinns in 1806, and by 1833 another new village was taking shape. Built with a view to exploiting lucrative fishing prospects, Port Wemyss was named after Walter Frederick's father-in-law, the 8th Earl of Wemyss. The site looked across to Orsay Island where, by 1825, a new lighthouse had been built to the designs of Robert Stevenson (some ten years after he completed the famous Bell Rock lighthouse). The base of the Orsay lighthouse was framed by typically Georgian buildings, a semi-circular store flanked by identical keepers' houses.

As at the other new villages, the elongated D-plan of Port Wemyss was also formal in composition and, whether or not by intent, the main axial street was aligned so as to frame a view of the new lighthouse. The original village was of mainly single-storey houses, tall enough to accommodate a loft, with two-storey houses lining the axial Main Street.

> *'The tenant to build a house according to the proprietor's plan, the tenant to furnish all the building material at his own expense, except the wood and slates, which were furnished by the proprietor at 7.5% per annum during the currency of the lease, a period of 99 years … the tenant … to keep the roof in sufficient repair at his own expense.'*
>
> Reverend John McNeill, Islay Free Kirk Minister, 1883

*Single-storey cottages lined the natural harbour, guarded by the newly built Orsay lighthouse.*

## Portnahaven

Portnahaven's naturally sheltered anchorage already supported a cluster of fishing families when Captain Walter Campbell took over the Sunderland estate from his father in 1814. In the 1820s, it was Walter's decision to clear the old settlement and to replace it with the crisp Georgian formality of Islay's other new villages. The house types were to be similar to those of Port Wemyss, their uniformity emphasising the horseshoe shape of the harbour.

By offering rights to build and long leases, Walter Campbell aimed to attract impoverished rural families and so free up farming land to increase the productivity of his estate.

Walter's plan for the village included several shops and an inn. Other community buildings, such as the church and the school were built inland from the bay to be accessible from neighbouring Port Wemyss.

# Keills

Traces of settlement suggest long and continuous occupation of this fertile plateau overlooking the Sound of Islay, but development into the village of today began with Walter Frederick Campbell in the 1820s. As part of his strategy for commercial diversification, he built five pairs of cottages at Keills to resettle skilled flax spinners and weavers from the mainland. As a small-scale enterprise, Islay's weavers were unable to compete with upcoming industrialised production and the industry dwindled. The cottages remain.

*Three of the semi-detached weavers' cottages built by Walter Frederick Campbell to attract skilled linen weavers.*

*Approaching Ballygrant from Bridgend in around 1900, with Miners' Row on the left, the tall back elevation of the former miller's house on the right and the other amenities beyond.*

# Ballygrant

Surrounded by fertile arable land, the name of the village Ballygrant translates into 'town of the grain' and, for some 300 years from the 1600s to the early 1900s, the local farming community brought their grain to its mill.

The other vestiges of past industry which lie scattered in the landscape around the village are all that remain from the mining of lead and other precious metals first recorded in the 1300s. Successive lairds were optimistic about the potential of Islay's mines and invested accordingly, but commercial success eluded both the Cawdor Campbells and the Shawfield Campbells. Although Thomas Pennant estimated a mining population of 700 in 1772, his host, Daniel Campbell the Younger, noted that the Islay mines were less productive than those elsewhere in Scotland.

When the Morrisons took on the lairdship of the Islay House estate in the mid-1800s, they too sought to develop the industry, and many of the buildings in present-day Ballygrant date from this period. By investing in housing and amenities, the Morrisons looked to attract mining expertise from elsewhere and so to increase productivity.

In the 1860s the former tacksman's house at Robolls, now the Ballygrant Inn, became home to a new mining manager, and Welsh names appeared amongst the occupants of Miners' Row, a new terrace built with access at both lower and upper levels so as to accommodate 16 families, eight on each level.

Another terrace, on the other side of the roadway through the village, included an inn, a post office and a baker's shop, and the now demolished miners' recreation centre.

# Bridgend

Bridgend lies on the banks of the River Sorn at the head of Loch Indaal, surrounded by the woodlands of Islay House. Picturesque gatehouses stand at each of the entrances to these plantations, which were once linked by a William Playfair bridge across the roadway from Ballygrant.

The placing and character of Bridgend stem from both its location and its role as an integral part of the Islay House landscape. It marks the crossing point of two historic routes, one leading around the shores of Loch Indaal, the other running north-east to Port Askaig. For centuries, livestock on the way to mainland markets passed this way, pausing in nearby pastures. Long before the construction of Bridgend, drovers sought refreshment from an inn served by a mill and brewhouse in the old settlement of Kilarrow.

All traces of Kilarrow, other than the graveyard, were cleared once the new commercial and administrative centre of Bowmore had been established. Unlike the rambling Kilarrow, the new village of Bridgend was to be scenic and limited in function, its buildings carefully placed to create a central marketplace.

In 1849, James Morrison, who was to buy the estate, spent a week's holiday at Bridgend's inn, and in the 1880s Arthur Barnard, writing his account of Scotland's whisky distilleries, found it to be a most 'picturesque hotel'.

In 1838, Bridgend was chosen as an ideal location for a branch of the National Bank of Scotland, founded in Edinburgh in 1825.

*Beyond the substantial riverside Georgian terrace, the inn (now the Bridgend Hotel) faced the village school across a small marketplace.*

*Port Askaig in 1900.*

# Port Askaig

From the earliest times, the narrow waters between Islay and Jura enabled a route across to mainland Scotland and regular ferries were already crossing the Sound of Islay from Port Askaig in the 1600s. Drovers were using this route to export the island's cattle, and by the late 1700s this trade was so successful that there were demands for more space to hold the waiting animals. In the early 1800s the number of cattle exported per annum reached over 3,000.

In 1765 Daniel Campbell the Younger established the first commercial ferry service between Port Askaig and West Loch Tarbert, and sought funding for a new quay, which was then built by his brother, Walter, in 1779. In 1825, the sailing packets were replaced by a wooden paddle-steamer, *The Maid of Islay*. As the services became more frequent and the boats increased in size, the gradual transformation of Port Askaig began. The quay projected further from the shoreline and the hillside was progressively gouged out to accommodate ferry traffic.

Meanwhile the buildings of Port Askaig changed very little. The low-ceilinged two-storied core of the present hotel probably dates from the late 1600s and, by the mid-1700s, Port Askaig inn or 'change-house' was well established, listed as one of 17 locations granted the privilege of brewing.

*The religious turbulence of the period is recorded in built form by the many varied churches and manses on Islay. Initially rooted in religion, a rich variety of different educational offerings were, by the late nineteenth century, assimilated into a nationwide school system.*

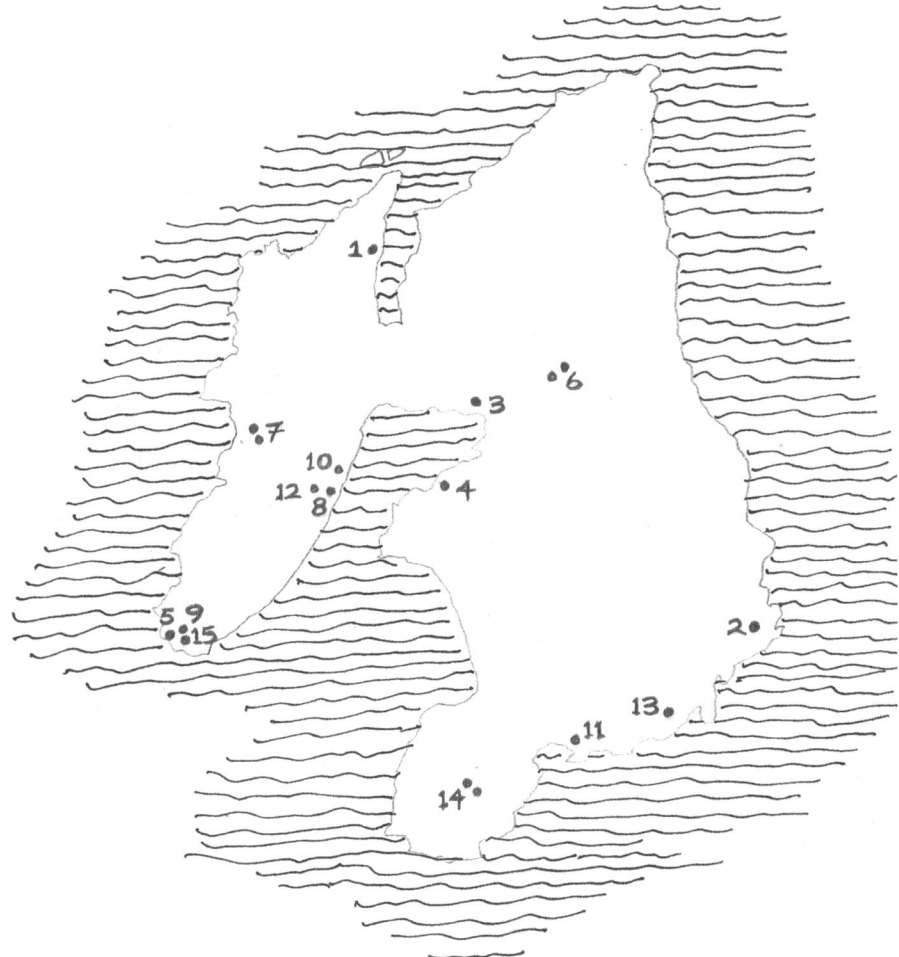

1. Kilnave Chapel
2. Kildalton Chapel
3. St Maelrubha Church, Maelrubha, Kilarrow
4. The Round Church (Kilarrow parish), Bowmore
5. Portnahaven Parliamentary Church
6. Kilmeny Church and Parliamentary Manse
7. Kilchoman Church and Manse
8. Port Charlotte Free Church
9. Portnahaven Free Church and Manse
10. St Kiaran's Church (between Port Charlotte and Bruichladdich)
11. St John's Church, Port Ellen
12. Port Charlotte School
13. Ardbeg School
14. Risabus School and Schoolhouse
15. Portnahaven School and Schoolhouse

# Churches, manses and schools

*The east window of the late medieval Kilnave Chapel.*

# Churches

Christianity arrived on Islay from Ireland in the sixth century, survived the Viking invasions and, once the invaders became converts, flourished again in the eleventh century. Conversion from Catholicism to Protestantism was to take a further six centuries.

Ruined places of worship are dotted across the island. At Ardnave the lands at Islay's north-western tip belonged to the Abbey of Iona until the late sixteenth century. One ruined thirteenth-century chapel (modified as a kelp-burning kiln in the late eighteenth century) stands on Nave island, another lies on the nearby shores of Loch Gruinart at Kilnave. The Kilnave ruins date from the fifteenth century, but a gaunt and weathered stone cross dating from the fifth century suggests a much longer history of sacred building on this site.

The fifteenth-century builders used thin slabs of local stone to form splayed, arched openings in walls nearly a metre thick. Internally there are signs of a plaster coating, but not of the fire that claimed the lives of Maclean warriors in the late sixteenth century. Lachlan Maclean of Mull had landed nearby, intent on ousting the MacDonalds of Islay. He died in the attempt and it was the Maclean survivors of the fierce battle who were burnt to death as they sought refuge in Kilnave Chapel.

At Kildalton on Islay's south-east coast, an exquisitely carved eighth-century cross, the best preserved *in situ* example in Scotland, stands beside the ruins of another early chapel. The original twelfth or early thirteenth-century fabric is similar to that at Kilnave, but altogether grander. Kildalton's relative size, complexity and embellishment with sandstone brought from the Mull of Kintyre, befit a place of worship close by the MacDonalds' seat at Dunyvaig.

Kildalton was still in use as a parish church when the Shawfield Campbells arrived on Islay in the early eighteenth century, as was the parish church of Kilarrow. However, when the latter was recorded by the artists who accompanied Joseph Banks' exploratory expedition to Islay in the late eighteenth century, their drawings show Kilarrow already in an advanced state of ruin.

Finding all of the island churches in a poor state of repair, and in exchange for taking over the ownership of Church lands, the incoming laird proposed funding a new era of ecclesiastical building. The first Shawfield laird was to die before he could fulfil his ambitions and the task fell to his grandson Daniel the Younger.

*The ruined thirteenth-century parish church of St Maelrubha at Kilarrow, drawn by combining information sketched in 1772 by the artists accompanying Joseph Banks. By then, the graveyard had been enclosed by walls and grand gateposts.*

In 1767, young Daniel completed the first part of his grandfather's ambition, the new Kilarrow parish church in Bowmore. For most on the island, this would have been the first sighting of such an elaborately stylish building and one devoid of all characteristics associated with earlier churches, a Georgian rejection of the medieval made manifest.

Whilst providing a necessary place of worship, Daniel also looks to have been showcasing his largesse and peerless architectural judgement. That there is no mention of an architect is not unusual for the Georgian period. The aristocracy regularly saw themselves as adequately conversant with the latest in theory and practice to direct the design process.

In this case, Daniel's close association with the 5th Duke of Argyll seems to explain where the idea for Bowmore came from. Sketches made for the 3rd Duke in the 1740s by William Adam show a circular church at the heart of the new town proposed for Inveraray. Later, more detailed drawings by William's son John show the Inveraray version as subdivided, with central, back-to-back pulpits addressing two semicircular spaces, one for the Gaelic-speaking congregation and one for the English.

The circular idea was eventually rejected by the 5th Duke, in favour of a subdivided rectangle, but seemingly found favour with the young Islay laird. In Bowmore the round form is arguably all the more impressive as it sits above eye level, literally crowning and adding grandeur to the gridded streetscape. The church itself works as a single unified space and the substantial entrance tower accentuates Bowmore's axial spine. The mason responsible for the finely carved sandstone was Thomas Spalding, a close friend of the laird, who settled on Islay and lived to the age of 105. He was buried at Kilmeny.

*Kilarrow Parish Church, Bowmore, 1767.*

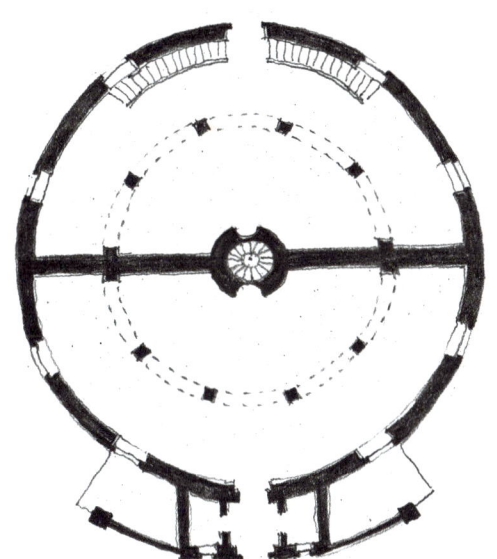

*The unbuilt Inveraray proposal by John Adam in 1758, based on his father's sketch from the 1740s.*

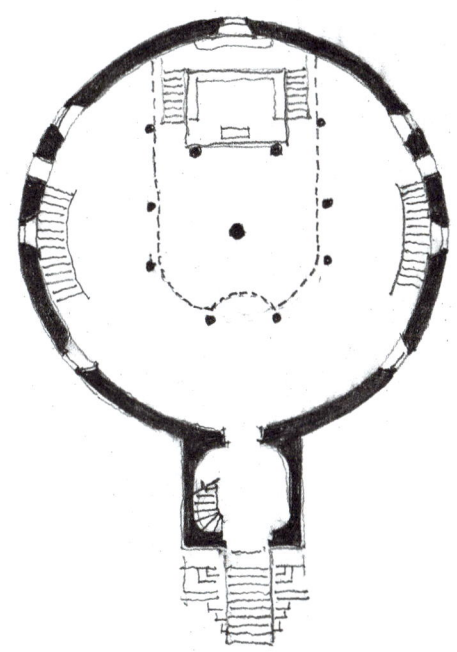

*The Kilarrow plan drawn to approximately the same scale.*

*The church at Kilmeny, built in the late 1700s to replace its nearby medieval forerunner, was remodelled in 1828 to the designs of Thomas Telford. The porch is a later addition.*

As part of the laird's same reconstruction programme, a new parish church replaced the nearby medieval chapel at Kilmeny, to the south of Ballygrant. This 1770s building was then remodelled some 50 years later by the 4th Shawfield laird, Walter Frederick Campbell, to tie in with a series of new government-funded buildings. In 1828, as an expression of gratitude for the successful outcome of the lengthy Napoleonic wars, Parliament commissioned a series of ecclesiastical buildings for parishes across the nation. The celebrated Scottish civil engineer, Thomas Telford, was appointed to produce standardised designs.

Around the same time, the established Church of Scotland was also investing in new buildings on Islay. At Kilchoman on the west coast, the old buildings were demolished in 1825 and work began on a new, particularly imposing church, and a nearby manse. Although now characterised by isolation amidst dramatic scenery, Kilchoman once sat at the heart of Islay's development, a powerful political centre favoured by island rulers until the seventeenth century. It was also the site of significant Christian activity, evidenced by the number of fifteenth-century carved stones in the churchyard. One, the Kilchoman Cross, is an impressive 2.5 metres in height and most elaborately detailed.

By the early years of the nineteenth century, the ruling lairds had long since moved away, but the population of Kilchoman parish stood at nearly 5,000. Serving this community as a place of worship and as a school called for a building of substantial size. Even today, in its ruinous state, Kilchoman church commands attention. It dominates the surrounding landscape and

*The 1820s Parliamentary church in Portnahaven.*

stands as a poignant reminder of the families who came from the surrounding countryside to form its congregation.

The rough stone walls of the church were once hidden behind the lime-washed, harled surface of the period, its geometry emphasised by buff sandstone dressings. Whilst the clean lines and decorative embellishments of the manse were entirely classical in origin, the pointed arches and slender buttresses of the church acknowledged an ecclesiastical gothic tradition. As the end of the Georgian period approached, the freedom to incorporate other than classical stylistic influences increased, typically so as to enrich aesthetic experience by evoking places or eras of relevance to the building's function.

The manse, Kilchoman House, nestles in a sheltered hollow to one side of the church. Equal in both size and refinement to the residences built by Islay's ruling class, it confirmed the status of the presiding minister. One of these, the Rev. Alexander Cameron achieved notoriety in the mid-nineteenth century because of an account of parish life. His openly critical appraisal of his congregation revealed his disapproval, amongst other things, of the way that they lived with their animals, their diet, their habit of gossiping and their moral shortcomings!

*Kilchoman House, dating from 1826.*

*Kilchoman Church, built in 1827.*

*The Free Church in Port Charlotte, built in 1843 and now the Museum of Islay Life.*

    The Rev. Cameron was one of many who left the Established Church of Scotland around this time. Unease about the extent to which the Church was controlled by central government and local lairds led to a schism. In what became known as the 'Great Disruption', a breakaway group formed the new Free Church of Scotland. This in turn led to a spate of new church building.

    In Port Charlotte the Established Church, recently built as a centrepiece by the laird, remained unused by a congregation who chose to shift their allegiance to the Free Church, building a new place of worship to the north of the village. Their first Free Church minister was to be Kilchoman's Rev. Cameron.

*The new Established Church closed the vista from the shore in 1830.*

The ensuing history of Presbyterianism in Scotland is complex. Whilst some like-minded worshippers came together as the United Free Church in 1900, others chose to remain separate and formed the Free Presbyterian Church, also known as the 'Wee Frees'. In Port Charlotte, this latest new congregation required yet another place of worship. Their church, now a house, stands close to the lighthouse to the north of the village.

In 1929 the United Free Church rejoined the established Church of Scotland, and although the 'Wee Frees' remained as a separate denomination, neither of Port Charlotte's Free Churches continued in use for much longer.

In Portnahaven, another Free Church building, dating from 1849, is typically low-key in size, form and absence of religious iconography. It could easily be mistaken for a functional extension to the adjoining manse, which was in fact added some 50 years later. The same building served the community as a Free Church School until the 1870s, when the government-funded school was built nearby.

*The Free Church and manse in Portnahaven.*

*St Kiaran's Church, which lies equidistant between Bruichladdich and Port Charlotte.*

*The effect of the red sandstone is best appreciated inside the church.*

In 1898, as a result of resettlement from rural crofting to village life, the Established Church at Kilchoman no longer lay at the centre of a community and a new parish church was founded, midway between the villages of Port Charlotte and Bruichladdich. St Kiaran's was designed by Peter MacGregor Chalmers, a well-respected and prolific church architect based in Glasgow. Peter started out as pupil of John Honeyman, best known for his partnership with John Keppie and Charles Rennie Mackintosh. Instrumental in developing the Arts and Crafts movement, the practice had a reputation for originality coupled with the fine craftsmanship they saw in buildings of the past. In particular they respected the honesty of medieval masons, where character resulted from structural and constructional necessity.

Shortly before designing St Kiaran's, Peter had carried out an archaeological survey of Jedburgh Abbey in the Scottish Borders. Built from local red sandstone, Jedburgh remains an impressive ruin, pared down to a skeleton which reveals the powerful robustness of arched and vaulted twelfth-century structure. At St Kiaran's, Peter chose a similar red sandstone, not for the whole building but to emphasise the arched construction around the doors and windows. Though much smaller and shaped to suit a more intimate space, these were built following the principles evident at Jedburgh, capturing its essence rather than mimicking its appearance.

*St John's Church, Port Ellen, designed by Sydney Mitchell and built in 1898.*

Settlement patterns on the east coast of the island had also changed significantly. Port Ellen had become the commercial and cultural centre for the Kildalton area, largely because of the success of the distilling industry. The earliest parish church, which still stands as a ruin at Kildalton, had been replaced, firstly in the 1730s and again in 1825. Then, in 1898, the Church of Scotland built the new parish church of St John's in Port Ellen.

The architect Sydney Mitchell came with a wide range of experience, having designed banks, hospitals and houses, as well as religious buildings. In 1883, his first commission, Well Court in Edinburgh's Dean Village, was much praised for pioneering a social housing typology. Today, it is recognised for its contribution to a particularly picturesque riverside setting. In a manner favoured by High Victorian society, Well Court combined elements borrowed from several different historic styles, but there, the over-rich complexity of eclecticism was skilfully unified by limiting the materials to a red sandstone and red roof tiles.

At St John's a similarly restrained material palette adds to the impression that the flowing form has been sculpted rather than assembled. The historic reference is said to be the French Romanesque church of Leulinghen-Bernes, and this could well be so, but this is a fresh interpretation rather than a copy. Formal borrowings are integral to the working of the building and fit seamlessly into the composition. The outward splay of the form as it meets the ground emphasises apparent weightiness and, although a small church, St John's is a monumental presence.

*The former Port Charlotte school.*

## Schools

Evidence of a commitment to education on Islay dates back to 1718 and to the establishment of a committee, made up of landowners and principal tenants, to oversee the distribution of monies to the island's churches, surgeons and schoolmasters. By the early 1800s, children across the island were attending lessons, mostly in churches, but also in private houses, some in Gaelic, and some in English. In addition to the four parish schools run by the Established Church of Scotland and supported by the laird, records show 28 other independent providers.

Walter Frederick Campbell, the 4th Shawfield laird, showed a particular commitment to education, funding school buildings for his new villages. A survivor from this period is the Port Charlotte school building, since used as a village hall, then housing. Designed originally as an Established Church but left vacant by a congregation who chose to join the new Free Church of Scotland in the 1840s, the building was extended and repurposed as a school.

As the century progressed, the number of education providers continued to increase, due partly to the split between the Established and Free Churches, and partly to the involvement of various charitable organisations. Most of the providers depended on the islanders' belief in the benefits of education. Even those on the most meagre of incomes found enough money to pay for their children to go to school. This they did and, in addition, they were expected to provide peats for the school fires.

*The typically symmetrical Ardbeg School – one side each for boys and girls.*

On the Kildalton estate, John Ramsay's first wife, Eliza, was clearly driven by the idea of education for all. In part, this was fuelled by the widely held belief that a firm grasp of the English language was required by those who wished to progress in life. One of Eliza Ramsay's projects was the building of a new school and teacher's house at Ardbeg, but she died in 1864 before she could see the completion of her achievements. Her choice of siting was particularly inspired, a rocky knoll which elevated the tiny school aesthetically as well as physically. The Ramsays and the Shawfield Campbells placed emphasis on the health benefits afforded by buildings of weathertight construction and ample ventilation, sited on well-drained, preferably elevated land. Eliza Ramsay's efforts are remembered in a plaque above the entrance to Ardbeg School, donated by Charles Morrison, by then laird of the Islay House estate.

Although the rural population declined following the lean years of the 1840s, several traditional settlements remained in Islay's south-east. At Risabus, on the Oa, the school and schoolhouse built by the Ramsays of Kildalton in the 1860s were sited alongside the earlier Parliamentary church and manse. The Risabus of today stands in isolation, and it is hard to imagine a time when it was surrounded by a vibrant community and when another three schools were required to serve this once populous rural area.

When free compulsory education was introduced in 1872, Islay already had about 30 schools. Gradually these were replaced by the education board's own purpose-built schools and school houses.

*The schoolhouse and school at Risabus near the ruined Parliamentary Church on the Oa, where they once served a substantial community.*

*Portnahaven School and schoolhouse date from 1878, and typify those built across the island following the Education Act of 1872.*

The school and adjoining schoolhouse at Portnahaven date from 1878, and typify the new buildings provided across the country following the Education Act. The architect, William Railton, had also designed a new school for Bowmore in 1876. Based in Kilmarnock and known for public buildings such as banks and hospitals, William was also a keen architectural historian, recording what remained of the castles in the south-west of Scotland.

His drawings focus on ruinous thick stone castle walls, and although the walls at Portnahaven are much thinner, he created apparent weightiness by boldly texturing the stonework. In character, this could not be further removed from that of Telford's Georgian church which stands nearby.

Although no longer used for education, schools from the late 1800s remain recognisable from the robustness of their construction as well as their formal symmetry. Most stand some distance from the villages, a reminder that despite the moves to rationalise agricultural production, many families were still needed to work the land before the advent of mechanisation.

*Intrinsically linked to the cycle of Islay life, industries based on water power were championed by successive landowners as a lucrative adjunct to agriculture, creating a unique architectural landscape.*

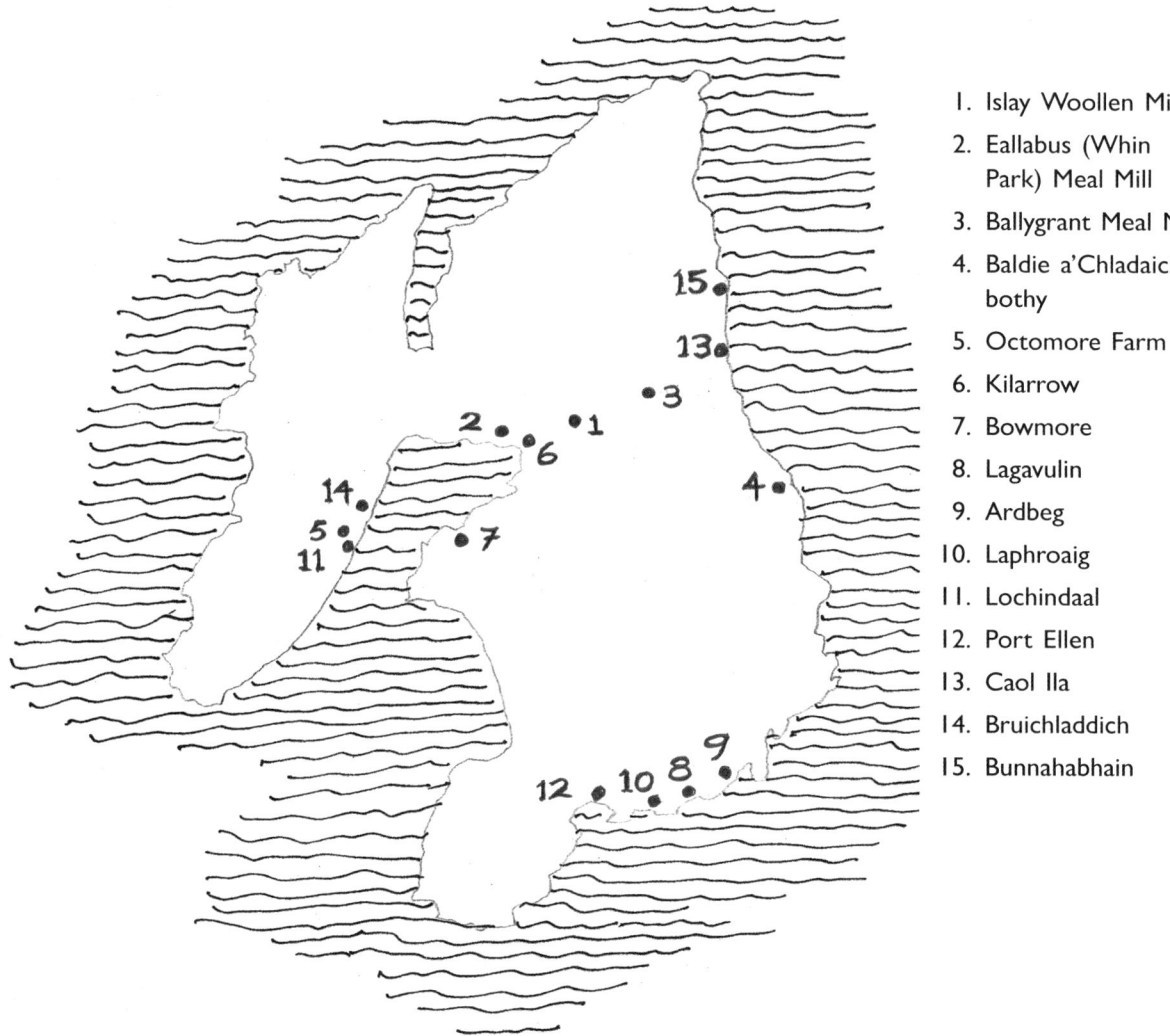

1. Islay Woollen Mill
2. Eallabus (Whin Park) Meal Mill
3. Ballygrant Meal Mill
4. Baldie a'Chladaich's bothy
5. Octomore Farm
6. Kilarrow
7. Bowmore
8. Lagavulin
9. Ardbeg
10. Laphroaig
11. Lochindaal
12. Port Ellen
13. Caol Ila
14. Bruichladdich
15. Bunnahabhain

# Mills and distilleries

## Linen (lint) and woollen mills

Commercial weaving was seen as worthy of investment by a series of Islay lairds. The production of linen from tall fibrous flax plants was long established on Islay when the 'Great' Daniel Campbell arrived in 1726. He aimed to increase productivity by building a number of lint mills, none of which survive. Successive Shawfield Campbells continued to support the industry, in part by encouraging experienced weavers to resettle in the new town of Bowmore. Although linen output peaked on Islay in the early 1800s, it quickly diminished in the face of competition from the industrial manufacture of cotton.

*The water-powered waulking, carding, spinning and weaving mill dating from 1883 lies upstream from the smaller, earlier mill building. The eighteenth-century bridge (shown in section) crosses the River Sorn between the two buildings.*

Islay also has a long history in the production of woollen fabric. The River Sorn, close by Islay House, was used to power both flax and wool processing. In 1658, Hugh Campbell of Cawdor installed a vertical waterwheel on the Sorn to power a woollen mill, probably on the site now occupied by later mill buildings.

Today, a bridge from the 1700s leads across the Sorn to two mill buildings. The smaller was built in the 1850s to cleanse (waulk) and disentangle (card) the fleeces ready for spinning. In 1883, the machinery from this mill was transferred to its larger neighbour, designed both to process fleeces into yarn and to accommodate looms for weaving blankets and tweeds.

'Great' Daniel Campbell's rigorously
Georgian grain mill near Islay House.

The Victorian meal mill on the site of
earlier mills in Ballygrant.

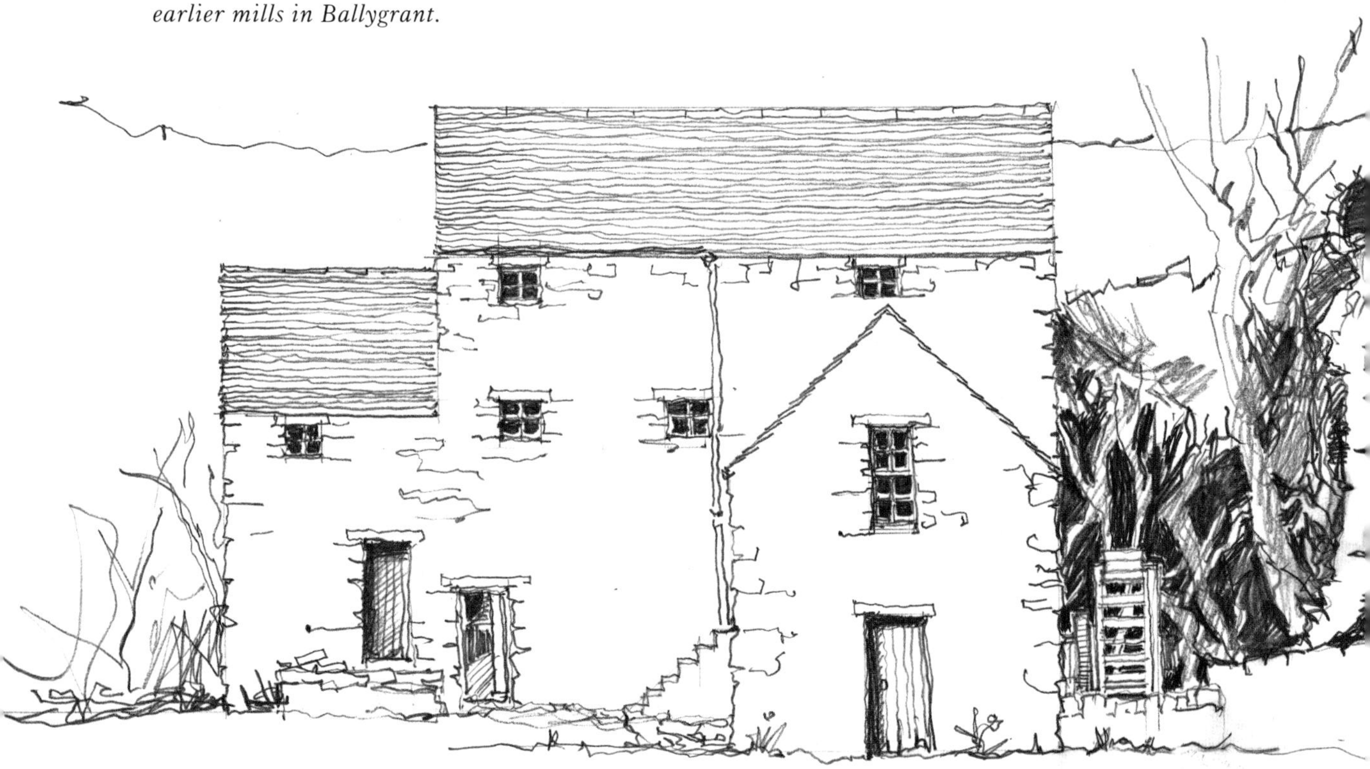

# Cereal crop (grain, meal) mills

In addition to investment in textile production, the Shawfield Campbells arrived on Islay with a view to increasing cereal crop yields, and the first laird built a sizeable mill for grinding grain close to his residence at Islay House. This was a truly grand Georgian mill with an air of refinement due to its well-proportioned symmetry, and must have been exceptionally impressive at the time of its construction.

In Ballygrant, part of a meal mill from the late 1800s, later repurposed as a sawmill, stands on a site where milling almost certainly predates records from the 1600s. The Victorian mill dates from a time when it was no longer *de rigueur* to disguise inner workings behind a façade, so it would have contrasted markedly with the formality of the Georgian example.

In the mid-1700s, 11 mills were listed as driven by vertical water wheels. Others, smaller in scale and built for more localised usage, were recorded as driven by horizontal waterwheels, and were known as 'clack mills'. These smaller horizontal wheels could drive millstones using lesser watercourses, and the more secluded of these played an important role in supplying widespread domestic distilling. Indeed, by the late 1700s, there are numerous reports blaming food shortages on the quantity of Islay barley feeding whisky production.

*Baldie a'Chladaich's home on the Sound of Islay. His whisky was made in one of the nearby caves.*

# Distilleries

Whisky taxes in Scotland were first collected in 1644, a system standardised and enforced by excise officers after the Act of Union in 1707. Islay was an exception. Here, the 'Great' Daniel Campbell, whose mansion in Glasgow had been besieged by malt tax protesters, was granted a personal right to collect excise duty. It would be nearly 150 years before an excise officer set foot on the island.

With abundant water, barley as a staple crop, peat as a ready fuel source, access to remote caves and an undoubtedly *laissez-faire* policing regime, it is no wonder that distilling took root so firmly. Neither is it hard to understand the attraction of malt whisky amongst the islanders themselves, or those who sought it out for entertaining in the grand houses across the nation. On occasions, the loose tongues of the latter were blamed for revealing secret locations when the excisemen finally arrived in the 1790s.

Around this time, the Napoleonic wars limited imports, poor harvests decimated local supplies and distilling was banned. In 1795, 90 stills were confiscated, but with little effect. Only six years later, another ban saw over 200 islanders charged with illegal distilling. Walter Campbell, the 3rd Shawfield laird, built a new brewhouse in Bridgend in an attempt to change drinking habits, again with little effect. The eminently portable distilling equipment in Port Charlotte's Museum of Islay Life shows how easily Islay's small-scale operations could elude capture.

*Octomore farm on the hillside above the former Lochindaal distillery, Port Charlotte. A plan shows traces of the distillery.*

| Islay distilleries licensed in the early 1800s: | | | |
|---|---|---|---|
| Ardbeg | Daill | Lagavulin (John Johnson) | Newton |
| Bridgend | Keppolsmore | | Octomore |
| Ballygrant | Kintour | Laphroaig | Octovulin |
| Bowmore | Lagavulin (Archibald Campbell) | Lossit | Tallant |
| | | Mulindry | |

By the early 1800s, the efforts of the excise collectors and a more favourable tax regime had made legal distilling more attractive. Even then, at least one of Islay's illegal distillers is known to have continued into the late 1800s. On one of the least accessible stretches of coastline, at the edge of the Sound of Islay, Baldie a'Chladaich's bothy is now a hikers' refuge.

One of Islay's earliest licensed enterprises started out in the old settlement of Kilarrow, where David Simpson is recorded as a farmer, merchant and distiller. By 1766, he had moved to Bowmore, and ten years later, with the new town rising around him, he began quarrying stone for the first purpose-built Bowmore distillery. In 1779, with the rights to 'win turf from the moss', his new distillery went into production.

Following tax revisions in the early 1800s, other distillers followed his example. Some developed alongside farming, some evolved from clusters of illicit production and some served inns. Some were short-lived, but the farm distilleries at Daill, Tallant and Octomore operated for 20, 30 and nearly 40 years respectively.

*The early Georgian buildings (with a later staircase) at Laphroaig.*

Of these early distilleries, those at Ardbeg, Bowmore, Lagavulin and Laphroaig emerged as the most successful. With ample water supply and quayside access, they were able to grow and thrive, gradually taking on the characteristics which came to typify commercial production.

Milling, malting and brewing are recorded at Lagavulin (the Gaelic for 'mill in the valley') from the early 1600s, and given that this is the site of Dunyvaig, stronghold of the MacDonald Lords of the Isles, beer and whisky would have been produced here long before. At least ten illicit bothies clustered in the valley, before two families, the Campbells and the Johnstons, invested separately in larger-scale legal production.

At Ardbeg, illicit production also predated the licensed distillery, which was established in 1815 by local farm tenant John McDougall. In the same year, another farming family, brothers Donald and Alexander Johnston, began commercial production at Laphroaig.

By the 1820s, whisky production had become a valuable source of employment as Islay's landowners looked to reduce dependency on agriculture. Walter Frederick Campbell, the 4th Shawfield laird, established distilleries in his new villages of Port Charlotte and Port Ellen. Both were located on sites with a long history of malting and milling barley.

The laird also leased land adjacent to Laphroaig for the construction of a rival venture. Adenistiel (later renamed Kildalton and then Islay distillery) was run by distillers from Clackmannan, James and Andrew Stein. The shared water source led to lengthy disputes, and by 1853, following the death of Andrew, Ardenistiel had ceased production. The buildings remain embedded in those of Laphroaig.

Founded in 1825, the Port Ellen distillery also struggled to make a profit until John Ramsay took charge in 1836 and introduced changes that would affect the industry as a whole. His was the first spirit safe, still a critical part of today's production, and Port Ellen was the site of Scotland's first duty-free warehouse.

Caol Ila dates from 1846. An established Glasgow distiller, Hector Henderson, recognised the potential of a cove to the north of Port Askaig, formerly known as Freeport. This had long been an industrial site, smelting and exporting the lead ore mined inland, and some of the existing buildings were incorporated into the new distillery.

*A typical nineteenth-century distilling process.*

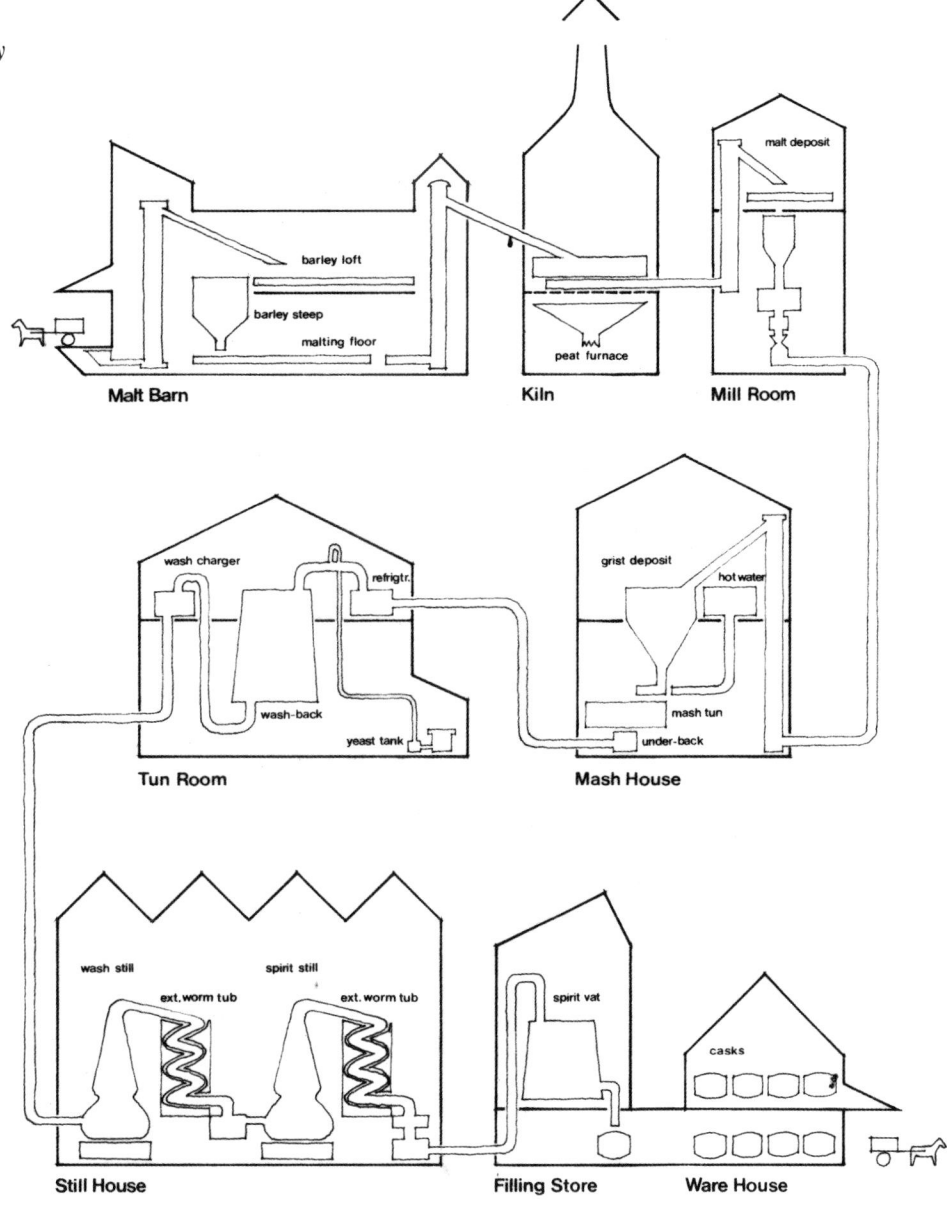

*The original 'pagoda' style kiln, still in use at Laphroaig, was invented by Elgin-based architect Charles Doig in 1889. It was widely adopted across Scotland, and proved highly effective in drawing smoke through the germinated barley whatever the wind direction, as well as keeping the rain out.*

Similar to the farm buildings of their origins, the thick rubble walls of the new distilleries were coated with harling and supported steeply pitched slate roofs. Imported cast iron enabled bigger spaces and heavier floor loading. Each distinct phase of the process called for an appropriate type of enclosure and the sequence of production dictated the way in which these were arranged in their particular landscape. Each of Islay's distilleries was therefore unique in its composition.

On the relatively flat site at Ardbeg, the buildings could be positioned to create sheltered working spaces between them. Two long, low malt barns, where the moistened barley was spread out and regularly turned to control germination, formed the east and west sides of a generous courtyard. From the barns, the barley moved into the taller, square kiln buildings, where peat smoke percolated up through mesh flooring to arrest germination. Infilling the seaward end of the courtyard between the kilns, a sequence of interconnected buildings housed milling, brewing and distilling. The final stage in the process, filling the barrels ready for export (prior to on-site warehousing) took place next to the new stone pier.

Although no longer all used for their intended purposes, Ardbeg's original barns, mash house, filling store and kilns have been retained throughout the distillery's subsequent evolution. The character of these may look familiar today, but at the time Ardbeg was pioneering the distillery typology which was to take shape across Scotland.

Alongside the distillery, the original farm buildings of Ardbeg stand as a reminder not only of the origins of distilling, but also of the reliance in the early days on an ample, local supply of barley. Also nearby, the distillery built workers' cottages, a shop, post office and grander homes for the manager and excise officer. In 1891, the Ardbeg school numbered 39 pupils, children from the distilling community.

Although developed at the same time, nearby Lagavulin seems comparatively haphazard. Irregular spaces and surprising changes in scale have resulted from the tightness of the valley site and from the distillery's origins as two distinct early enterprises.

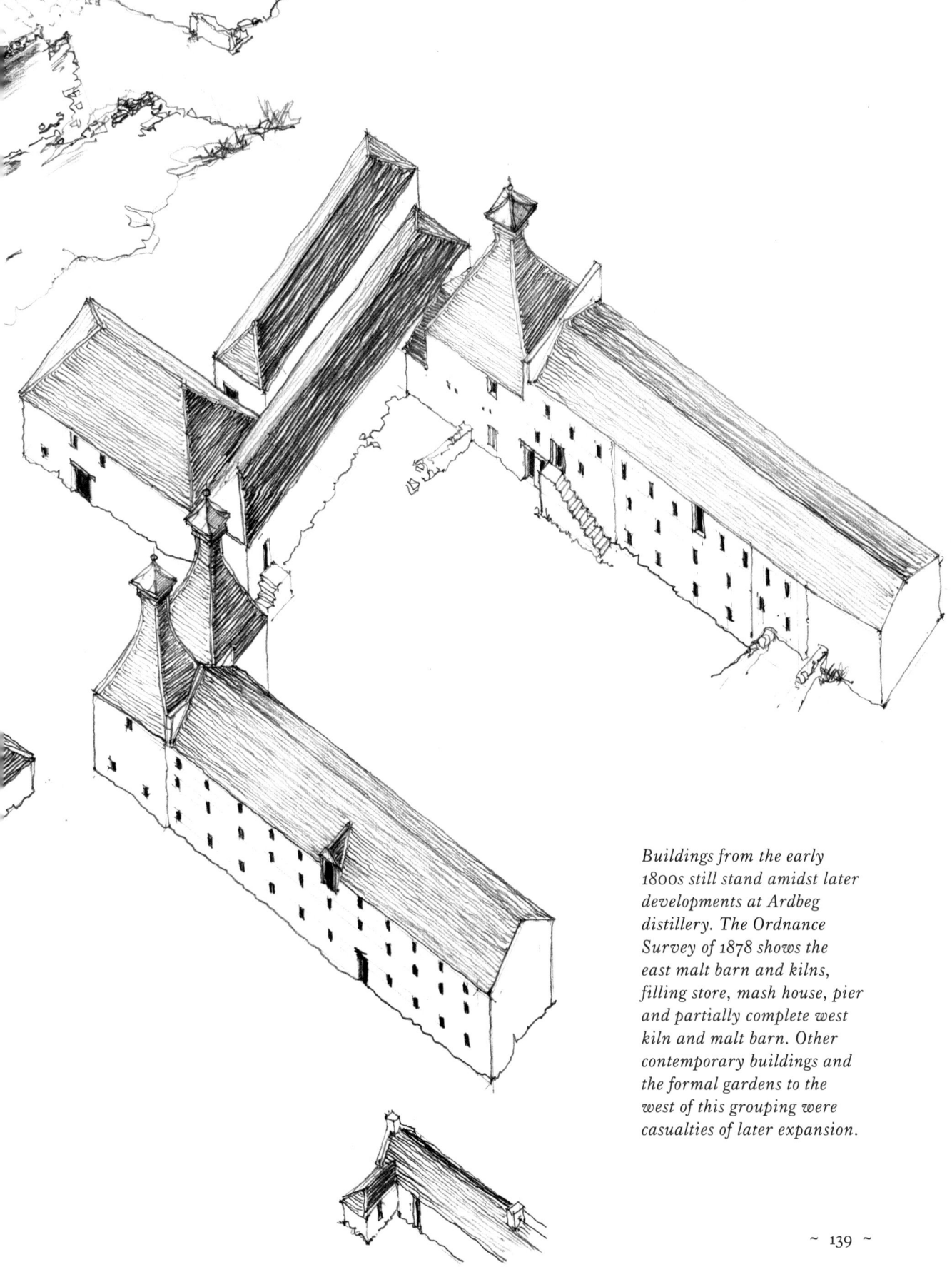

*Buildings from the early 1800s still stand amidst later developments at Ardbeg distillery. The Ordnance Survey of 1878 shows the east malt barn and kilns, filling store, mash house, pier and partially complete west kiln and malt barn. Other contemporary buildings and the formal gardens to the west of this grouping were casualties of later expansion.*

*The Malt Mill buildings within Lagavulin.*

*Lagavulin distillery in 1870, tightly packed into the valley, with early rotatating 'cowl' ventilators and a waterwheel.*

By 1837, the distilleries founded by the Campbells and Johnstons had amalgamated. Then, in 1878, a young Peter Mackie arrived at Lagavulin, becoming a partner to John Graham, whose family now held the lease. Peter began to develop the art of whisky blending, producing the famous White Horse brand by 1891. Later, in 1908, he built again on the Lagavulin site to make a whisky similar to Laphroaig. Known as Malt Mill, production of this whisky continued until the 1960s. Interestingly, it was quite distinct in flavour, unlike either Lagavulin or Laphroaig.

One of the most demanding of the sites was that at Caol Ila, where the distillery tumbled down towards the water's edge. Enlargement in the 1970s required wholesale demolition and regrouping into a single, glass-fronted shoreside building. As at a number of other Islay distilleries, the traditional

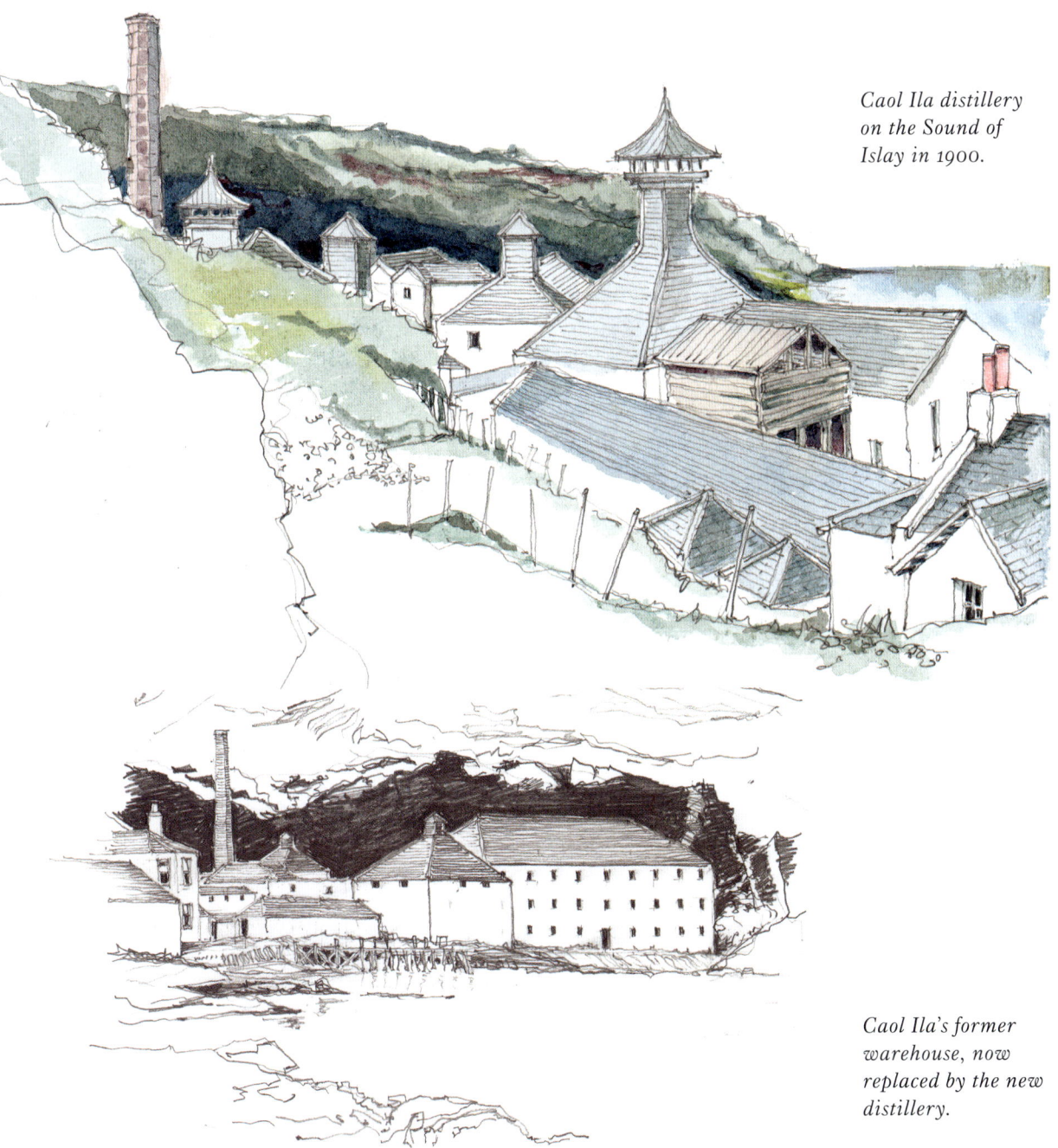

*Caol Ila distillery on the Sound of Islay in 1900.*

*Caol Ila's former warehouse, now replaced by the new distillery.*

malt barns and kilns were no longer required when the mass-production of malted barley was established in Port Ellen. Monumental in scale, one of Caol Ila's warehouses still stands at the shore's edge. It would dominate most settings, but here, nestled into the tall dark face of the hillside, it simply holds its own.

The buoyant state of the industry on Islay was recorded by Alfred Barnard, whose book *The Whisky Distilleries of the United Kingdom* was published in 1887. On Islay he visited all nine distilleries: Ardbeg,

*Bowmore distillery in the 1880s, with its tall, tapering rotating ventilators (left-hand side of image) to the newly built kiln houses – similar to those on oast houses. The shoreside still house was Georgian in style, with generous, arch-topped opening windows.*

*By 1900, the two kiln houses had been heightened and topped with the latest 'pagoda' roof ventilators, the still house doubled in size, and warehouse capacity increased.*

Lagavulin, Laphroaig, Port Ellen, Caol Ila, Bowmore and Lochindaal, as well as two new ventures at Bunnahabhain and Bruichladdich.

By the time Barnard visited Bowmore, Islay's first licensed distillery had already undergone constant transformation from its humble beginnings, growing and modernising to meet demand. Barnard's account illustrates its spacious still house and newly built malt kilns, but an image from 20 years later shows that expansion was continuing apace.

Built in 1881, Bunnahabhain and Bruichladdich took advantage of fresh water supplies and navigable quaysides. Whilst individual elements in the distillation process remained recognisable, the virgin sites enabled an

*Bunnahabhain distillery.*

integrated whole, organised to maximise efficiency and security. In both cases, linked buildings formed a sheltered courtyard, entered though a single gateway.

At Bunnahabhain, both its gateway and bulky austere buildings are well suited to the remote expansive landscape of Islay's north-east. Bruichladdich, on the low-lying arable shores of Lochindaal, is altogether less formidable, and sits comfortably at the heart of the village which grew around it.

Although driven by practicalities rather than any stylistic intent, the relationship between these early industrial buildings and the landscapes around them remains one that is undoubtedly rewarding. Viewed from land or sea, we recognise the kind of mutual enhancement of buildings and landscape that is probably best described as truly picturesque.

*Bruichladdich distillery.*

# And a small but significant building ...

*The Sanaig water-closet, front elevation and (right), section.*

In 1828, George Leitch married Catherine McMillan in the modish and pristine Kilchoman church. George came from a large farming family and had grown up at Kindrochid, a relatively small holding on a hillside to the north of Loch Gorm. In 1824 the records name ten tenants as sharing the rental (including three branches of the Leitch family), double the number recorded 20 years earlier. As a boy, George would have witnessed his father John's arrest for illicit distilling.

In 1841, George was appointed as sole tenant of the much larger farm at Sanaigmore, an example of Walter Frederick Campbell's policy of promoting those whom he saw as enterprising.

In April 1847, the *Exmouth*, a ship heavily laden with impoverished Irish farmers and their families sailing for Canada, sank off Islay's north-west coast. Of the 240 on board only three survived. The islanders buried 108. A memorial at Sanaig records the tragedy, as do watercolour sketches by John Francis Campbell, Walter Frederick's son, which show islanders pulling bodies and debris from a deep gully. Given the proximity to Sanaig, this event would have impacted deeply on George and his family.

That same year brought the potato blight to Islay, a dismal summer affected other crops, livestock prices continued to fall and the bankruptcy of the Shawfield laird brought the termination of leases. On 21 November 1847, George, Catherine and their nine children, in full and terrifying knowledge of the potential dangers involved, boarded a similar vessel to the *Exmouth*, also bound for Canada. Their ship landed safely, and the family, along with most of their relatives, settled into a new life in Glenelg, Ontario.

Only one branch of the family stayed on Islay. Daniel Leitch made a new life at Knockdon, tending the sheep imported by William Webster, the interim manager of the Islay House estate.

The house at Sanaig has since been demolished, but the remains of a little stone building perch over the nearby burn, somewhat chillier but undoubtedly more scenic than the water-closet installed by John Ramsay at his first Islay residence, Cornabus, around 1830.

# In conclusion

*One (certainly not the last) iteration of Lochindaal distillery – as youth hostel and garage – the rusty corrugated-iron roofs a reminder of wartime utilitarian repurposing, literally layered onto the remains of buildings which tell the story of another era.*

*Of the nine distilleries described by Barnard, only Lochindaal distillery in Port Charlotte is no longer in production today, pictured here as a ruin in 1979.*

'When we build . . . let it not be for present delights nor for present use alone. Let it be such work as our descendants will thank us for.'

JOHN RUSKIN

'Let us by all means exploit the wonderful opportunities which our new materials and new techniques have placed in our hands; but let us also be vigilant for our inheritance.'

ALEC CLIFTON-TAYLOR

'For stories and buildings alike, incremental change has been the paradoxical mechanism of their preservation . . . Architecture is all too often imagined as if buildings do not – and should not – change. But change they do, and have always done. Buildings are gifts, and because they are, we must pass them on.'

EDWARD HOLLIS

# Bibliography

UNPUBLISHED WORKS
Leitch, D. M., 'Islay Distilleries', University of Newcastle School of Architecture Thesis, 1974.

PUBLISHED WORKS
Barnard, A., *The Whisky Distilleries of the United Kingdom*, Edinburgh, 2003.
Caldwell, D. H., *Islay, Jura and Colonsay: A Historical Guide*, Edinburgh, 2011.
Caldwell, D. H., *Islay – The land of the Lordships*, Edinburgh, 2017.
Gordon, J., *The Machrie Links*, Edinburgh, 2023.
Gregory Smith, G. (ed.), *The Book of Islay*, 1895. Reprinted Colonsay, 2010.
Islay Association, *The Kilchoman People Vindicated from the Charges of the Rev. Alex Cameron*, 1867. Reprinted 2018.
Jupp, C., *The History of Islay from Earliest Times to 1848*, Port Charlotte, 1994.
Lindsay, I. G. and Cosh, M., *Inveraray and the Dukes of Argyll*, Edinburgh, 1973.
MacKechnie, M., *The Lords of the Isles and the Roots of Scotland*, Islay, 2018.
Mackenzie, R., *Agriculture on Islay*, Port Charlotte, 1990.
Minto, J. and Wilson, L. (ed), *Islay Voices*, Edinburgh, 2016.
Mithen, S., *Land of the Ilich: Journeys into Islay's Past*, Edinburgh, 2021.
Ramsay, F., *The Day Book of Daniel Campbell of Shawfield, 1767*, Aberdeen, 1991.
RCAHMS, Argyll Volume 5, *Islay, Jura, Colonsay and Oronsay*, Edinburgh, 1984.
Storrie, M., *Islay, Biography of an Island*, Islay, 2011.
Walker, F. A., *The Buildings of Scotland: Argyll and Bute*, Yale, 2000.

ELECTRONIC SOURCES
Bell, Catriona, Ballygrant and Keills – a glimpse of the past. Available at: *https://islay.scot/* (accessed January 2024).
Bonehill, J., The Artist as Eye-witness: Joseph Banks, John Cleveley and the Millers, Old Ways New Roads: Travels in Scotland 1720–1832 (2021). Available at: *https://www.gla.ac.uk/hunterian/* (accessed January 2024).
British Library. Available at: *https://www.bl.uk/* (accessed March 2023).
Canmore. Available at: *https://www.canmore.org.uk* (accessed January 2024).
Campbell, W., Earl, M., Mackay, F., Macphail, C., Mcqueen, F. F., Islay, A Local History Project by the Isle of Islay Federation, Scottish Women's Institute (1968). Available at: *https://islay.scot/* (accessed January 2024).

Carmichael, G., Macaffer, F., MacEachern, P., Old Islay. Available at: *https://www.facebook.com/groups/445628108785691/* (accessed January 2014).

Ramsay, F., John Ramsay of Kildalton. Being an account of his life in Islay and including the diary of his trip to Canada in 1870 (1968). Available at: *https://archive.org/details/johnramsayofkild00ramsuoft/page/n5/mode/2up?view=theater* (accessed January 2023).

Walker, D. M., Hillyard, Y., Harris, L., Grater, A. (compilation), Dictionary of Scottish Architects 1660–1980. Available at: *https://www.scottisharchitects.org.uk/* (accessed January 2024).